the foot book

THE FOOT BOOK

by Dr. John Lazar, D.P.M., R.Ph.

Dry Bones Press, Inc.
P. O. Box 1437
Roseville, CA 95678
http://www.drybones.com
(415) 707–2129

Publisher's Cataloging–in–Publication Information
Lazar, John —
The Foot Book / by John Lazar
72 p. cm.
Index included.
ISBN 1–883938–96–1
1. Foot—care and hygiene. 2. Foot—popular works. 3. Foot.
4. Foot—anatomy. 5. Foot. 6. Podiatry
I. Title II. Author

RD563 613.4

Dedication

**To my wife, Ann,
and my daughters,
Jacqueline and Jenny Lynn,
who gave me the needed support to
make this book possible.**

Contents

Appendices

Introduction

While we could not do without them and use them all the time, we tend to take them for granted: our feet. They are a miracle times 2, composed of 26 bones each, four layers of muscles, and a unique connection of 33 joints bringing into play many tendons and ligaments.

Despite the tremendous importance of the feet, we usually abuse them until they hurt enough to finally get our attention. Take care of your feet, and you will get more mileage out of them.

One purpose of *The Foot Book* is to help you understand common foot ailments and show you how to treat them simply at home. Another purpose is to help you understand more advanced treatments that a doctor may need to provide.

It is not the intent of this book to substitute for a doctor's care and treatment, but rather to help you understand the more common conditions of the feet. In addition, anyone with a debilitating disease such as diabetes should consult his or her doctor before attempting any treatment on their own.

A word about health professionals. A podiatrist is a specialist trained in the medical treatment and surgery of the foot. There are other practitioners who treat the feet and foot conditions. Whatever type of professional you consult, remember that an ethical doctor does not guarantee a result when it pertains to the human body.

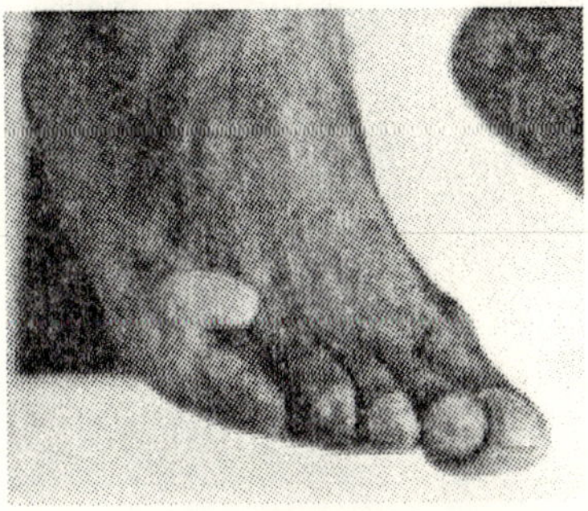

A finding of a sixth toe on each foot is normal for some patients,

ABOUT THE AUTHOR

John Lazar has always believed in good nutrition. He is very much a leader in a natural and holistic approach to treating medical problems and has focused that approach in his medical practice.

He is a doctor in the health field: that is his profession. He is an educator: that is his avocation.

John Lazar holds bachelor of science degrees in both pharmacy and social science and has been active as a registered pharmacist and as an educator in the pharmacy industry. He is also board-certified, with a doctorate in podiatry, and has practiced for more than 10 years in many capacities, including private office, group medical, hospital and residency teaching, and HMO practice. In addition, he is an inventor and holds a U.S. and Canadian patent on a medical device for the feet.

Dr. Lazar feels that *The Foot Book* will help bring the reader knowledge that will enhance the quality of their health and lives.

Chapter 1

site of vulnerability
Toenails

Each toe, like each finger, has a nail, and toenails are one of the most exposed, and so one of the most vulnerable, parts of the feet. Toenails crack and split, just like fingernails. Two of the most common maladies of the toenails are well known: ingrown toenails and fungal nails.

INGROWN TOENAIL

If you're like most of us, you have experienced the discomfort, or more likely, the downright pain, of an ingrown toenail. This common problem affects almost everyone, especially children and adolescents, whose bodies are growing and changing rapidly.

ingrown toenail
FACTS

- **Ingrown nails are a normal part of growing up. Most occur before age 18.**
- **The big toe becomes ingrown about 10 times more often than the other toes.**
- **Many newborns suffer ingrown toenails.**

What Is an Ingrown Toenail?

Toenails cover the nail bed, the skin on top of the toe. The nail fits into skin folds or slots on the left, the right and the base. If the nail does not fit well in the slots and there is a tear in the skin folds—because of a bump to a side of the nail, improper cutting of the toenails or picking at them (a favorite habit of some people)—an ingrown nail can develop. It also may be a natural result of growing up and changing nail shape.

Signs and Symptoms

The first symptom of an ingrown nail is pain at the nail corner, possibly accompanied by redness, often seeming to develop overnight. Examine the nail closely. Does one particular place hurt most?

In severe cases, the skin at the nail corner may be raised and possibly reddish or bluish. This is the full-blown ingrown nail, with infection extending outside the immediate nail corner. The raised area contains pus, a fluid indicating infection, which may be draining.

Home Care: Soak!

If the problem seems contained to an area near the front of the nail, trimming the nail might solve the problem. Use a standard nail clipper, trimming straight across to prevent recurrences. But if the area is infected—swollen, red, painful draining pus—*soak!* Soaking softens the skin around the infected area and helps loosen the nail, moving it away from the skin, thus lessening the pain. It also can draw out the infection, kill germs and keep the infection from spread-

TRUE CASES

- **In the worst case of ingrown nails, the patient was diabetic, with all 10 nails ingrown.**
- **Severe infections may**

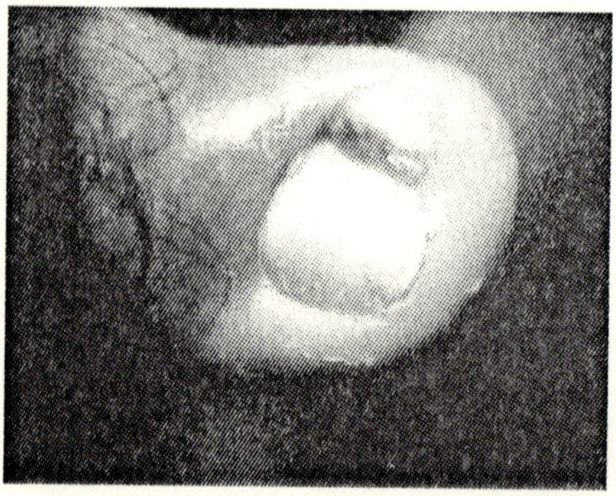

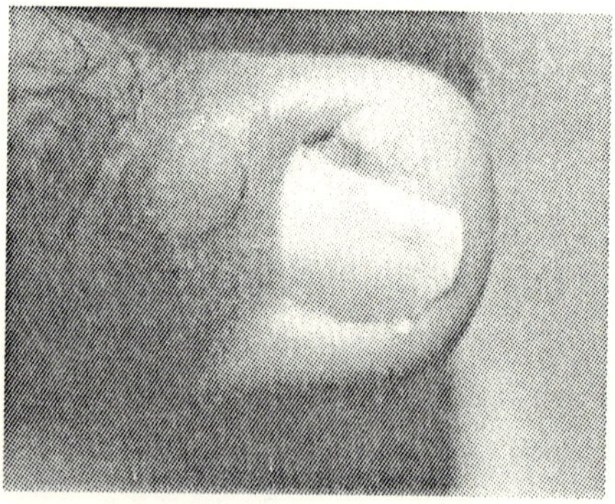

An infected swollen ingrown toenail (left) before surgery. Note the additional overgrown skin of the nail border. A corrected ingrown toenail (right), two weeks following surgery. Note the smooth skin of the nail border.

ing.

Either of two common household substances—white vinegar (which contains acetic acid) or chlorine bleach (known chemically as sodium hypochlorite, *never used together*—can sometimes take care of the problem. Add 1 oz. of either substance to 1 gal. of warm *not hot* water, and soak the affected toe for 20 minutes twice a day. (Hot water can damage the sensitive, infected area.) For maximum safety, sterilize the water by first boiling it for 20 minutes, then allowing it to cool to a comfortable warmth.

After Soaking

To soothe the inflamed area after soaking, and to continue to treat the infection, apply an antiseptic solution or cream. *Povidone-iodine* solution kills germs, helps dry up the skin and promotes scab formation and faster healing. *Triple-antibiotic ointment* or other nonprescription antibiotic cream will help relieve the pain and continue to kill germs when you are on the go.

Wear loose gauze or an extra-wide strip bandage to prevent the sore toe from rubbing against your shoe and to avoid staining your sock and shoe.

When to Seek Professional Care

Home care should help most ingrown nails, but if the pain and infection do not improve even slightly within 72 hours, seek professional advice. Left untreated, a seriously ingrown toenail can result in cellulitis, in which the infection spreads to the foot or ankle, requiring hospitalization. Be alert.

For the serious ingrown nail, a professional has a choice of treatments. First, an X ray can determine whether the infection has reached the bone (the bones themselves can become infected). If infection has not progressed to the bone, the offending nail corner might be surgically removed and allowed to grow back. If the problem continues to repeat itself, the professional might recommend permanent removal of the root of the affected edge of the nail. This procedure, called matrixectomy, is usually done by laser, which sterilizes the area, causes little discomfort and promotes rapid healing.

NAIL FUNGUS

You've seen the pictures, even if you haven't seen the real thing. Toenails yellowed, crumbling, split and flaking, thanks to infection by a fungus. The fungi are a group of plantlike organisms that includes mushrooms, yeasts and molds. The fungus that affects the nail works its way to the moist, dark nail bed, where it thrives. Yeast infections may also infect nails.

Nails disfigured by a fungus not only look ugly, they harbor an infection that may spread to family members, where it can affect their nails—or cause athlete's foot. The two maladies are caused by the same fungus! Swift treatment is a good idea.

nail fungus
FACTS

- **A variety of related fungi can cause crumbling nails.**
- **Fungus grows deep under the nail and can spread from person to person.**
- **The fungi are a widespread group of plants**
- **An antibiotic eyedrop, Gentamicin, can kill fungus on the nails.**

Home Care

Home care starts with keeping the nail fungus from spreading to others. It is a good idea not to pick at your toenails. Not only could this expose your nail bed to the fungus, it also causes the nail to flake, putting others at risk. No one should use your towel or washcloth if you have a nail fungus.

Treatment isn't easy. External remedies—antifungal creams and solutions—do not work unless they penetrate the nail. And people with diabetes and those whose skin is naturally alkaline will have a harder time combatting the fungus than others. There is an external topical nail lacquer called Pen-Lac (ciclopirox 8% topical solution), available by prescription only, that works well in some cases. It can be used for Diabetics also.

A first step is the old-fashioned white-vinegar soak, 1 oz. of white vinegar to 1 gal. of warm water, 20 minutes twice a day. This mildly acidic solution can help keep both fungal and yeast infections at bay.

When to Seek Professional Care

If home treatments and soaks do not bring a fungal infection into check, or if the nail becomes ingrown or painful, consult a podiatrist.

The professional may remove the affected nail under local anesthetic,

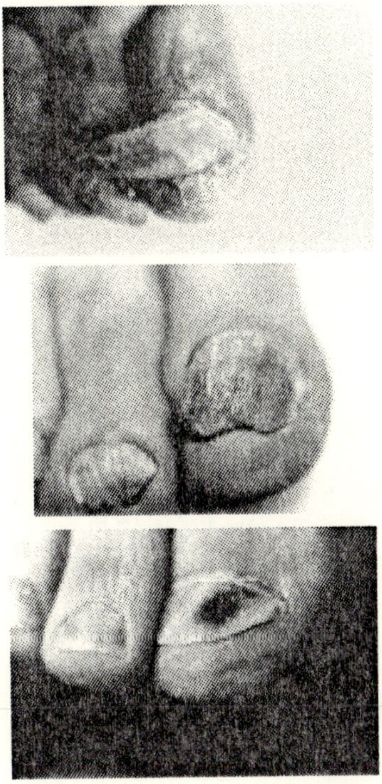

A toenail severely infected by fungus (top, left); note additional fungal skin underneath the nail. A variant fungus causes a blackened toenail (center); note that the skin beneath the nail is not affected. Another variant fungus causes spotty black coloration (bottom, left) without affecting the skin.

Dramatic improvement in nail quality (below) after taking oral prescription antifungal medicine. Note the lighter color and better texture at the cuticle, in contrast with the old, darker nail at the tip.

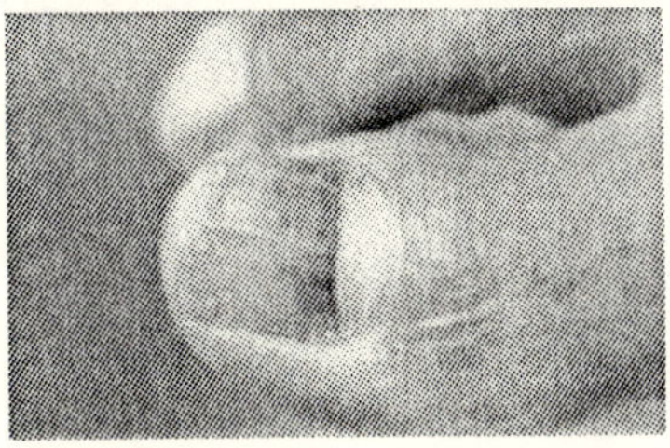

then treat the nail bed with an antibiotic and possibly use a laser to kill the fungus and yeast. In some cases, treatment may include an oral antifungal drug.

Such drugs are taken concurrently with or before surgical treatment. Because the medicines are digested by the liver and may overload it, the liver function is monitored monthly with a simple blood test.

Nail fungus can be persistent. Treatment may take as long as a year, and 50 percent of the infections are never cured.

Nail Irregularities

From time to time you may see lines, ridges or bumps in your nails. They usually indicate nothing more serious than a poor diet. Occasionally, however, they result from diseases of the liver, digestive system or urinary tract.

For irregularities caused by diet, gelatin capsules and a good multivitamin with the essential amino acids will usually help. Remember that it takes 60 to 90 days to grow a completely new nail, and it might take that long to see a change. If the lines are severe and do not seem to improve, consult an internist or a podiatrist.

TRUE CASES

- **The worst patient with fungus not only had all fingers and toes affected, but also the skin of the feet was infected with fungus up to the ankles.**

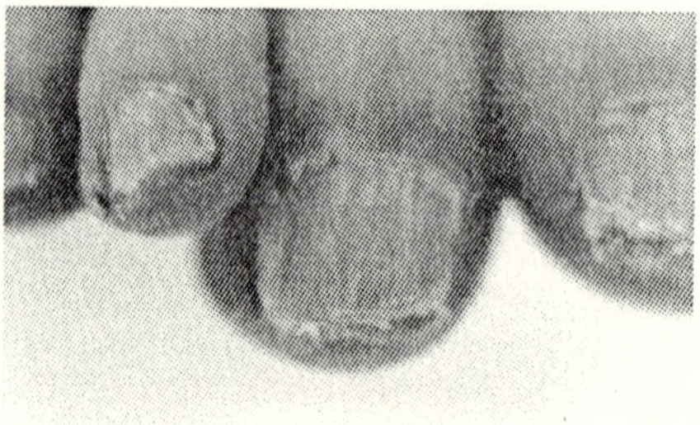

Lines or grooves in the nails can be temporary or permanent, depending on the cause.

Chapter 2

Skin

Remember: Your feet are covered with a "bootie" of skin. And this skin isn't just one layer thick. There are actually seven layers—three thicker, deep, living layers, and four outer, dead layers.

Just like skin on your face, hands and body, the skin on your feet needs proper treatment. That skin is subject to many of the same problems as skin anywhere—plus a few that are unique to feet.

> **skin of the feet**
> **ODDITIES**
>
> - **Some rashes are caused by an allergy to the shoe material and match the shoe's outline perfectly.**
> - **It's rare, but insect bites on the foot have caused such a severe infection that the foot had to be amputated.**
> - **Someone who sweats excessively, even in winter, can develop parakeratosis.**
> - **Foot fungus can be made worse by too much sugar or fat in the diet.**

WORKING UP A SWEAT

It's no surprise: Our feet sweat--a lot! The soles of the feet have more sweat glands per square inch than any other part of the body. So it should be no more shocking to learn that sweating is the culprit in many foot ailments, providing bacteria and fungi the perfect environment. For diabetics it's even worse: Glucose, or sugar, in the sweat makes feet even more appealing to microbes.

You can attack the sweat problem in several ways. Wear socks made of a thick, absorbent material, such as cotton. Select white socks when you can; they don't contain dyes, which can cause allergies. Buy leather shoes, which provide adequate breathing for the feet; synthetic materials are less porous. Never wear the same pair of shoes two days in a row. Alternating lets the previous day's shoes dry out. Take off your shoes during the day if you can, to give the feet some fresh air. And on off days, apply powders or other formulas (see the Dry Recipes, page 88) to the inside of shoes to help freshen them and stop bacteria and fungi.

A good tonic for the feet is a soak in warm water containing three tea bags. The tannic acid in the tea has a drying effect.

ATHLETE'S FOOT

If you've never had athlete's foot, surely you know someone who has, and chances are he or she wasn't an athlete—anyone can get it.

Athlete's foot, or technically, *tinea,* is a fungal infection of the skin of the foot. This annoying problem can become serious if not treated promptly. As in fungal nails (page 12), fungus can penetrate the deeper layers of the skin, causing peeling and flaking off of the outer layers.

The fungus can survive only in the living, deeper layers, where it can get nourishment from the body. Because the infection is deep, treatment must be persistent to reach all affected layers. Even a minor bout of athlete's foot will require two weeks' treatment, while more serious infections take longer to treat.

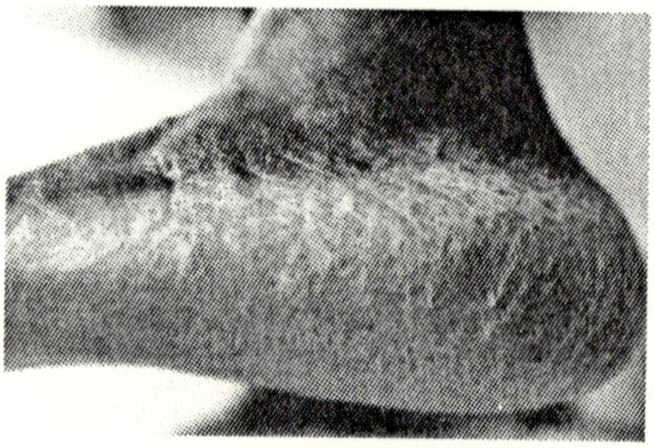

Severe, long-neglected athlete's foot can mimic a "moccasin-like" rash.

Initial Treatment

Soak the feet in white vinegar or a dilute sodium hypochlorite solution (add 1 oz. of chlorine bleach to a gallon of water). Soak 10 to 20 minutes, morning and night, for two weeks.

Many effective antifungal creams are available. Use any one of them after soaking. Apply lightly, then rub it in well—but rub gently to keep from injuring the affected skin, which could encourage further fungal growth.

Deeper infections might warrant a nonprescription antibiotic dressing, such as Bacitracin or triple-antibiotic ointment. Apply after bathing, and cover with a loose sterile bandage.

If the depth of a fungal infection increases, see your doctor.

Longer-term Infections

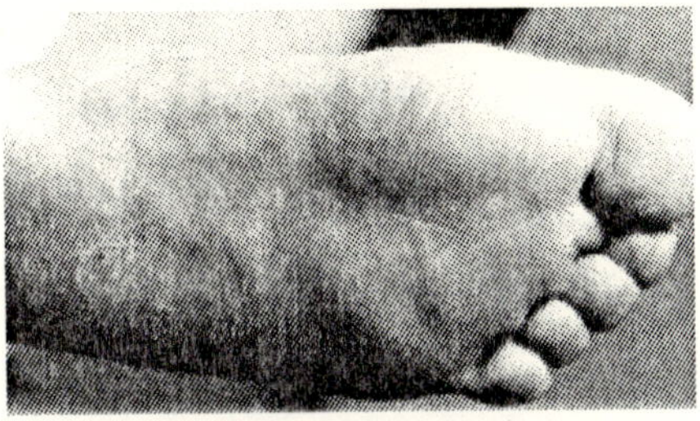

Unchecked fungus of the sole can result in multiple fissure-like cracks in the skin.

If a fungal infection is neglected for a long time, it may appear as a vertical crack or fissure in the skin, especially on the heels. This usually indicates that the skin has been infected for more than a year, and such a long-term infection might take another year to eradicate. Try soaking with Betadine (Povidone-Iodine) solution at 1 ounce per gallon of water for 10 to 20 minutes. Continue the soaks for two weeks. Betadine can be purchased at any local pharmacy without a prescription and is more effective than vinegar or chlorine.

In persistent cases, your doctor can prescribe oral medication to treat the cracking fungus-affected skin.

Prevention

It is a good idea never to walk barefoot, especially in the street, but even in your own backyard or around a swimming pool. You have no idea what creepy crawlers might have slithered by overnight and left behind contaminants lying in wait for your feet. If you do go barefoot, wash your feet with an antibacterial soap as soon as you are inside.

Use an antifungal cream to treat an existing infection. Use an antifungal powder to maintain clear skin.

Wear thick white socks, which have no dyes that might cause allergic reactions.

ALLERGIC DERMATITIS (ECZEMA)

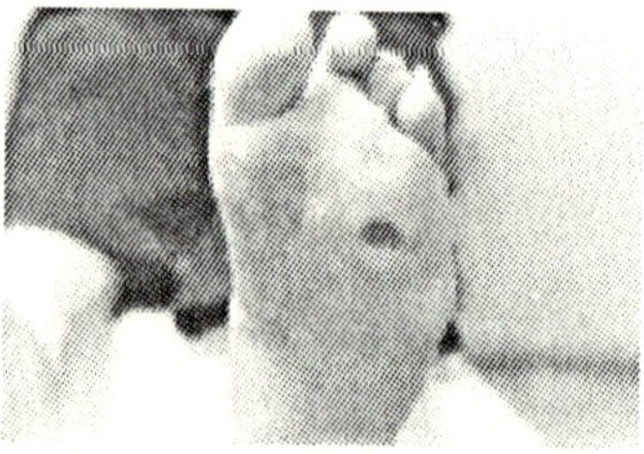

Eczema can result from temporary irritation or an allergy to a substance.

Inflammation of the skin due to an allergic reaction is called *allergic dermatitis,* a description that includes a broad range of conditions and treatments.

For minor skin irritations, allergic rashes and insect bites, choose from a host of nonprescription cortisone creams. These products range from ½% to 1% hydrocortisone creams and ointments, which may also contain emollients such as aloe and lanolin.

A severe allergic reaction to a drug, called the Stevens Johnson Syndrome. This reaction can affect the entire body and is self-limiting. The outer dead skin will shed, and new skin will develop slowly.

In case of minor infection, with accompanying local redness, soreness or tenderness, use any of the nonprescription antibiotic ointments or creams and cover with a loose sterile bandage or bandage strip. Apply twice a day until the symptoms subside.

If pus is leaking from the affected area, a deeper infection has developed. See a doctor for a prescription for oral antibiotics.

WARTS

Like cold sores in the mouth, warts are caused by a bloodborne virus that creates a raised area of skin that can be quite painful. They are common on the feet, but unfortunately, where they might spring up is not predictable.

On feet, warts occur most often on the sole, or *plantar. Plantar warts* usually extend much more deeply into the skin than warts elsewhere on the foot. That's not unusual, because the skin of the sole is much thicker.

The wart has its own skin lines, different from those of the "footprint" of the surrounding normal skin. This is a key characteristic in distinguishing a wart from other skin problems.

A wart appears as a tiny round red pimple but grows larger and deeper. It is painful if you grab it with two fingers and squeeze the sides. (If it hurts only when you push directly down on it, it is probably a corn or a callus.)

Closer observation reveals tiny black dots in the middle, and sometimes minor bleeding.

the skin of the feet

WARTS

- **If warts are bleeding, they can be spread by contact.**
- **Warts can result from viruses that live on the skin of some animals.**
- **Warts grow so deep that the virus enters the blood and can spread to other parts of the body.**

Home Care: Nonprescription Treatments

Warts are difficult to treat, because the virus cannot be seen. Nonprescription wart medications and medicated pads use acids to destroy the skin and can be dangerous if used improperly: They can destroy adjacent unaffected skin as well. However, they can be effective for small warts if used properly. Be careful to apply the medication only over the limited area of the skin affected by the lesion. Likewise, cut medicated pads down so they fit the exact size of the wart, not extending over unaffected skin.

Use these products exactly as directed. Allow enough time between applications to allow the skin to breathe and to prevent total breakdown of the skin. Misuse can result in an infec-

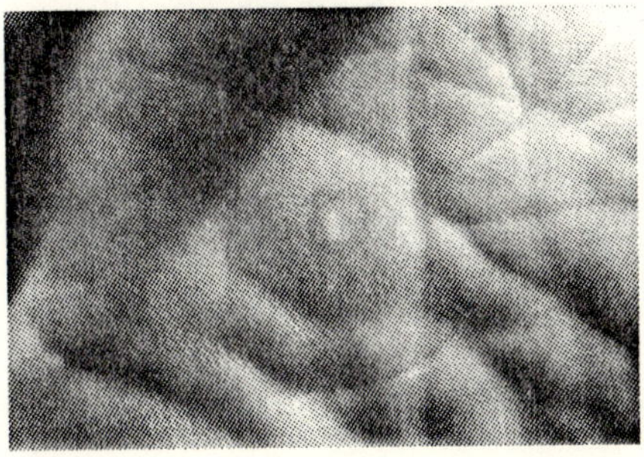

A plantar wart on the sole can mimic parakeratosis; note the absence of skin lines in the lesion and its smoothness.

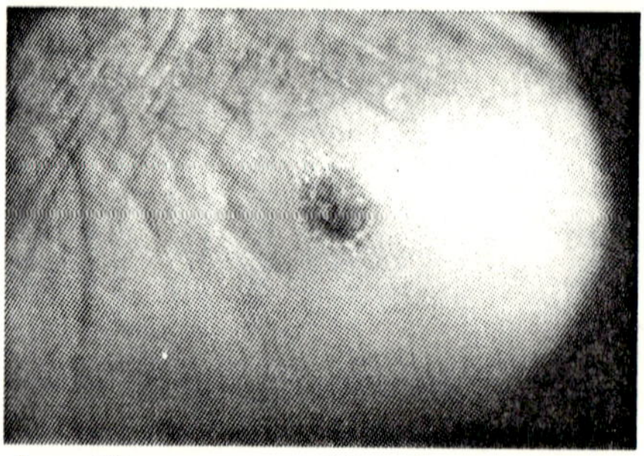

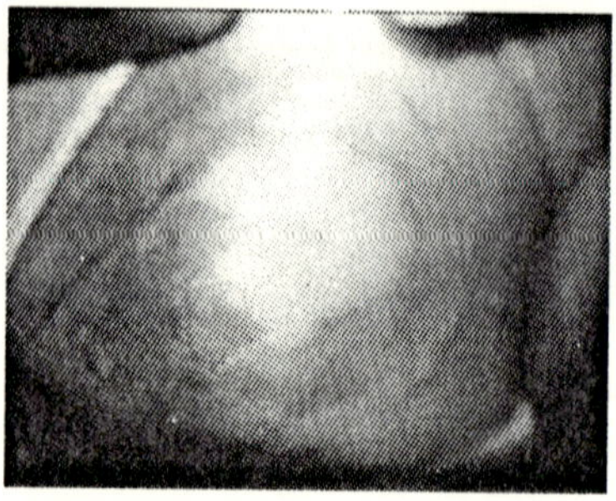

The classic signs of a wart (left). The scattered black dots in the lesion are tiny blood vessels. The same area, after the wart was removed in the office by nitrogen freezing (cryosurgery). Note that the local area has newly formed skin and is lighter in color. This will blend in naturally over 6 to 12 months.

tion. If an area of skin changes color or enlarges quickly, consult a professional.

A Doctor's Care

Beyond the small-pimple stage, warts are usually difficult to remove yourself. Doctors have several ways to tackle a more advanced wart.

They may excise it under local anesthetic, stitch the affected area, and allow it to heal. Stitches are removed in 10 to 14 days, with complete recovery in a couple of weeks.

On the soles, excision can result in a scar that can cause pain during walking. For plantar warts, a CO_2 laser is better. The affected tissue is burned away or vaporized, also under a local anesthetic. Healing time varies with the size of the affected area.

Liquid nitrogen is a third method, similar to dry ice, usually applied without anesthetic. Liquid nitrogen is a very cold liquid that is applied directly to the wart with a small cotton swab in order to freeze off the wart. The nitrogen causes the wart to blister, and then to dissolve or fall away in about a month.

Remember, because warts are caused by a bloodborne virus, they might recur in the same spot or in a different location.

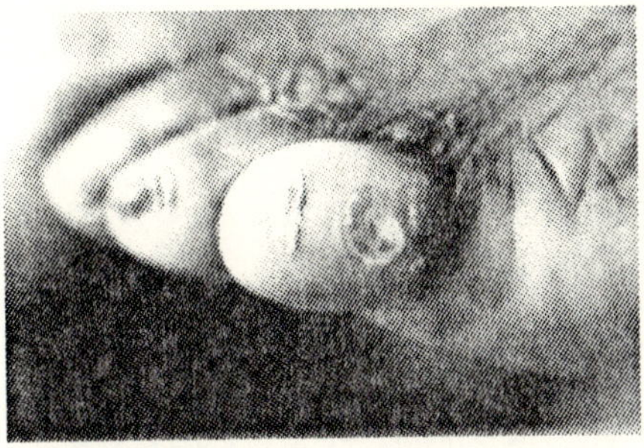
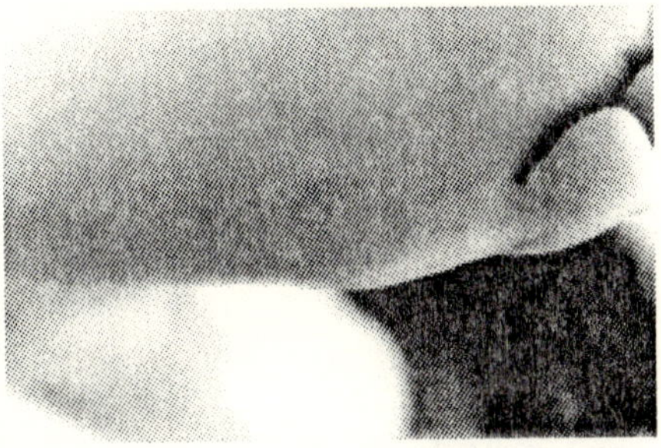

Corns (left) are thickened normal skin tissue caused by rubbing action in tight shoes and commonly occur on little toes. Calluses can form anywhere on the soles and are caused by constant rubbing, such as under the little toe metatarsal bone shown here (bunionette).

CORNS AND CALLUSES

A thickened area of skin that doesn't hurt when pinched is probably a common benign corn or callus. (If pain results only from direct pressure, the thickened area is probably not a wart.) A corn and a callus are two forms of the same thing: thickening of the skin. Calluses are larger and especially likely to form on the bottom of the feet. Corns are smaller and most often form on the top of the toes; in fact, corns may be described as calluses of the toes.

In both calluses and corns, the "footprint" lines of the surrounding skin do not change, so the thickened area blends in with the surrounding skin. (This is a way in which calluses and corns may be distinguished from warts, where the surrounding skin does change; see "Warts," above.)

Calluses and corns have the same cause, or *etiology*: pressure against the bones of the foot—

corns and calluses
FACTS

- Corns and calluses don't have a central root.
- Corns and calluses occur only as a result of a bone disorder.
- Our bodies are actually encased by layers of dead skin! The living skin lies deeper.
- The worst callus ever seen covered the entire sole of the foot.
- Use a worn, soft toothbrush to safely clean scaling skin from between the toes.

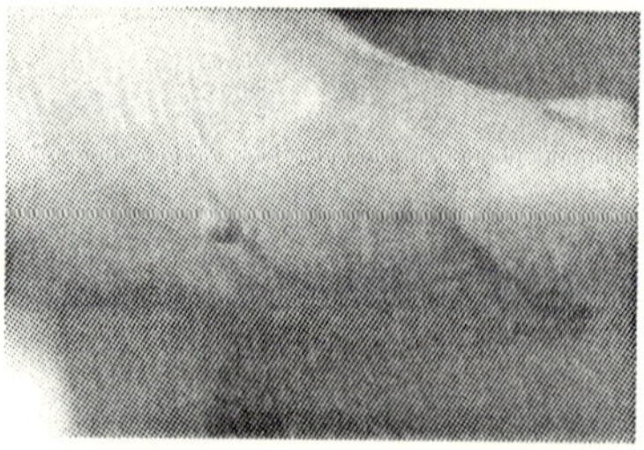 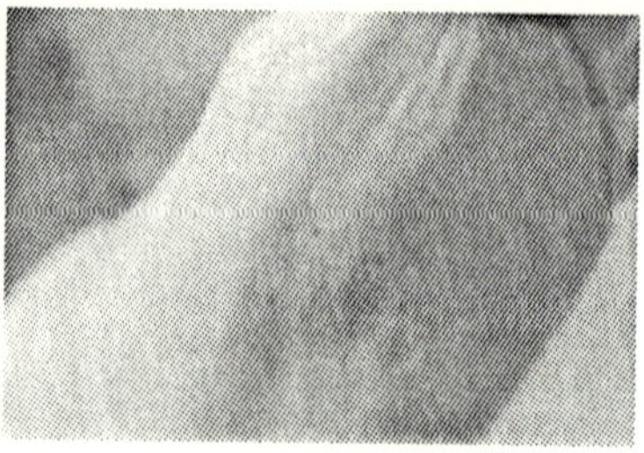

A "skin tag" (left), an uncommon growth of the foot, is painless and benign, but annoying in shoes. The same area (right) in close-up, after the skin tag was surgically removed in a simple office procedure. The mass was classified as a "fibroepithelial polyp," a benign skin tumor.

whether from walking or a displaced bone pressing against the inside of a shoe.

Calluses are common under the long bones of the forefoot, the *metatarsals*. They are the body's means of protecting these bones during walking. Yet calluses sometimes become so thick that it can hurt to walk or even stand up. This can cause the normal skin beneath the callus to break down and crack, become preulcerous, and be susceptible to infection.

The most well-known cause of corns is a shoe that is too tight or that cocks a toe into a claw-like position, which creates unnatural pressure at a joint. Due to constant rubbing, the skin thickens and develops into a corn.

There are two types of corns. *Hard corns* are found on the outer surfaces of the toes and feet. *Soft corns* are found between the toes (soft because they are often wet from the sweating between the toes). The most annoying soft corns develop between the last two toes, at the base of the web. Corns come in all shapes and sizes, but they generally become no wider than the toe itself.

As with calluses, pain from corns comes from the excessive pressure the corn causes.

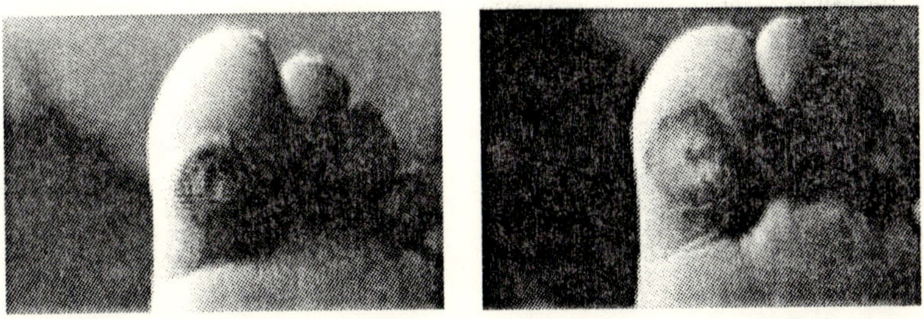

A seemingly innocent callus (left) of the great toe can cover and hide a perforating ulcer of the skin often caused by diabetes. Careful debridement of the surface skin reveals an ulcer (right) forming beneath the callus.

Treatment

If you determine that you have a simple corn or callus, you often can treat it yourself. However, because both calluses and corns may become preulcerous and thus open to infection, they could prove devastating if you have a debilitating condition such as poor circulation or diabetes. In those cases, seek professional treatment even for simple corns and calluses.

For the rest of you, treatment involves simply scraping and filing down the callus or corn using a pumice stone (actually lava rock), or off the shelf callus removal tool and scraper, available at any pharmacy. However, the affected area is usually dry and scaly, and not easily removed. So, first soften the skin by taking a shower or soaking the foot in warm water for 10 to 20 minutes. If you like, use the *vinegar-and-water solution* described previously in this book.

Once the area is softened, scrape off the dead thickened skin by rubbing the pumice stone repeatedly over the area until the thickened skin seems to have disappeared and your natural skin color returns. After you have performed this treatment several times you will get a feeling for how much to scrape off and be able to do it without hesitation.

After this treatment the area will probably be a little sensitive. Apply a piece of felt or moleskin, available in most pharmacies, for a day or so.

Soft corns between the toes are comfortably relieved by wrapping

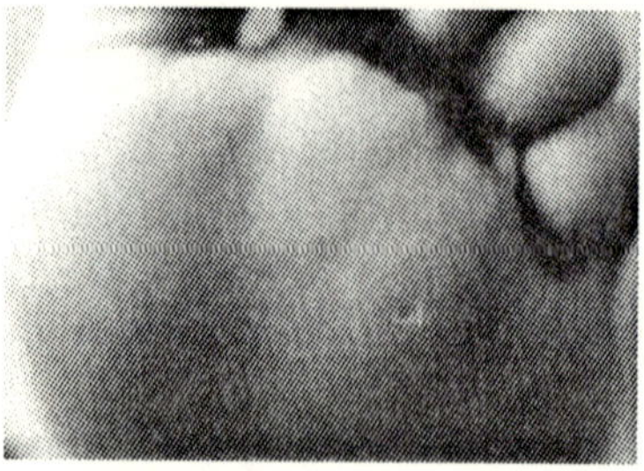

A parakeratosis can form anywhere on the sole, usually as a result of previous local trauma to the skin and its underlying tissue.

lamb's wool around the webbed base of the toe to soften the rubbing action between the toes. Lamb's wool, also readily available, looks like strands of hair and can be wound together in a ropelike fashion.

PARAKERATOSIS

Sometimes masquerading as a callus or a wart is the common skin condition of the feet called *parakeratosis*. The feet, of course, have sweat glands, which can become plugged with dirt or debris. As a result, the area enlarges and is painful to squeeze, like a wart. However, unlike a wart, these areas have the same skin lines as the surrounding skin.

This benign skin condition also may be treated at home. Treatment involves the use of acid pads, as described for the treatment of warts. Cut the pad to the exact size of the affected area, and change it every few days until the area is no longer elevated and side-to-side squeezing no longer produces pain.

PSORIASIS

A rash on the foot, usually on the parts of the foot that do not support

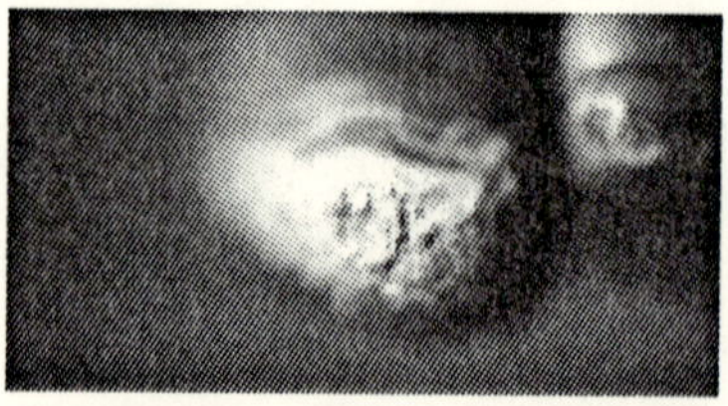

Psoriasis can attack many areas of the lower extremity. Here the great toe is chronically affected, resulting in severely thickened skin.

your weight when you are standing or walking, might be the fairly common disorder known as *psoriasis*. Symptoms of this hereditary condition include a rashlike area, rough in texture, with irregular borders and a silvery color. (This harmless silvery color, which results from tiny air bubbles trapped in the skin, helps distinguish psoriasis from other skin diseases.) The area is very itchy and persistent and will spread on all sides.

On the feet, the rash appears most often under the arch and on the top and sides of the foot. It can occur elsewhere on the body, such as the hands.

the heartbreak of
PSORIASIS

- **The most common symptom of psoriasis is severe local itching.**
- **Even the worst case of psoriasis does not involve the palms and the soles.**
- **The cause of psoriasis is not known, and neither is a cure. However, symptoms can be relieved in most cases.**

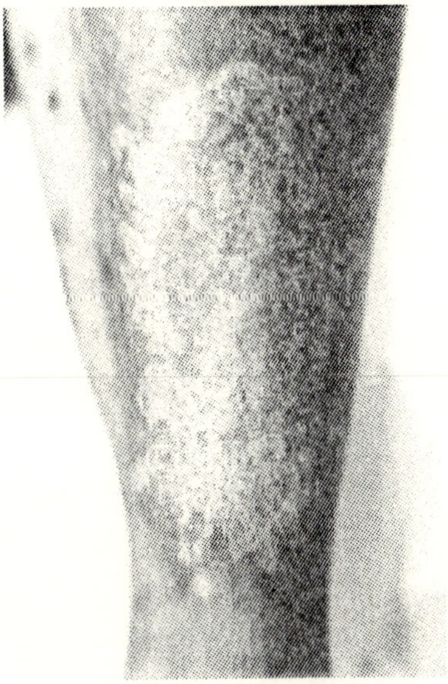

A classic photograph of a large psoriatic rash of the front of a leg. The telltale white glistening flaking skin can become quite pruritic.

Treatment

Psoriasis is difficult to eradicate, in part because its exact origin is unknown. However, it is thought to be brought on by chronic stress coupled with the virus that causes the childhood disease chickenpox. After chickenpox disappears, the virus resides in the nervous system, and the psoriasis rash forms along nerve lines.

While full treatment may take as long as a year, some topical creams have shown good results. They can relieve the itching in just a few days, which decreases the threat of infection due to breaks in the skin from scratching.

Coal-tar-based creams and lotions are

available without a prescription; talk with your pharmacist. A prescription is required for similar creams containing steroids. An alternative therapy involves prescription creams containing vitamin D.

Apply the cream twice a day after soaking in the white-vinegar/warm-water bath (see *Athlete's Foot,* page 16). A soak prepares the skin for the tar cream by lowering the pH of the area (making it more acidic), by cleansing the skin of natural oils and debris, and by opening the pores. After the symptoms and rash have disappeared, occasional use can help prevent the their return.

Creams applied to the skin cannot get to the root of the problem: stress. So it is a good idea to evaluate the sources of stress in your life and work at lessening it, which can make recurrences of psoriasis less likely.

SKIN BEAUTY AND WRINKLES

Aging is a topic that interests everyone, probably because it affects us all and cannot be ignored. In the quest for the most beautiful and wrinkle-free skin, there are too many so-called remedies to count. Knowing more about them can help you evaluate and select the ones most likely to help keep your skin in good condition.

Skin-care agents can be categorized into *creams* or *ointments*. Creams are less oily than ointments and are more likely to be better for your skin. They are called *noncomedogenic,* which means they are formulated not to clog pores or cause acne blemishes.

hope for
WRINKLES

- **Wrinkles are caused by lack of nutrients in the skin and by genetics too, not just by aging.**
- **Moisture can help to stop wrinkling.**
- **Nonnatural (nonorganic) foods and preservatives can increase wrinkling.**

Look at the Products You Already Use

The first step in evaluating skin creams is to look at the brands you are now using. If they burn or sting or in any way cause discomfort, they are probably bad for your skin. The burning indicates that the cream is not pH balanced or buffered. The ideal pH is neutral, 7.0, or slightly lower (slightly more acidic). Read the product label to determine whether the manufacturer has adjusted and buffered the pH.

A common ingredient in skin creams is *alpha-hydroxy acid,* which is heralded as a great skin reconditioner. But if the cream stings it can harm your skin and contribute to wrinkles rather than help. A good, buffered product has a neutral pH and does not feel uncomfortable.

Read the Label

Another good way to evaluate a skin cream or ointment is to study the ingredients, which are listed on the side panel or label. Some of the ingredients will be long words and difficult to pronounce. But look for basic signs, such as natural vegetable-based creams rather than fatty acids. Avoid ingredients with acids in their name and look for natural vitamins such as A, C, D, E and F. Creams containing these vitamins are considered antioxidant creams and are probably the best formulas for improving skin texture and color. Stay away from oily substances on the face, such as cocoa butter and waxes, and from lotions containing alcohol. Alcohol tends to sting and to dry the skin.

Instead, look for ingredients that hold water and transfer it to the skin. Such ingredients are called *humectants* and *emollients*. One example is pure glycerin, a liquid.

Natural protein replacement can help the skin maintain its youthful, healthy appearance. As we age, we gradually lose the protein beneath our skin, called *collagen,* which helps keep the skin spongy and soft. As collagen is depleted, the skin takes on a flatter appearance and begins to wrinkle. Another approach to skin care and wrinkle control, then, is the use of collagen-based creams to replenish the natural protein aging takes away.

Use common sense. Look at the label, and if you can't pronounce it, don't use it.

SUNBURN

When you hit the beach, you wear a hat, smear zinc oxide on your nose and cheeks and slather sunscreen across your shoulders--but what about your feet? They need protection too.

Despite the appeal of a suntan, exposure to the sun is dangerous, causing painful sunburn, blistering and peeling, and eventually resulting in leathery skin, wrinkles and a greater risk for skin cancer. Protect yourself, and don't ignore your feet.

Of the light that comes from the sun, the ultraviolet rays are the harmful ones. They are beamed from the sun in three wavelengths, UVA, UVB and UVC. UVC is blocked by the atmosphere and you do not need additional protection. Sun blocks and sunscreens come in a variety of creams, lotions and ointments that are available at most drugstores and supermarkets, and they protect from UVA and UVB rays.

All manufacturers' products are ranked by sun-protection factor, or SPF, which indicates the level of protection, the larger numbers (45 is highest) meaning more protection.

Use a sunscreen rated at least 30SPF, and apply it evenly over all exposed parts of the body—including the tops of the feet and between the toes. If the soles or other parts of the feet and toes are exposed when you lie down, apply sunscreen to them too. If you plan to swim or expect to sweat a lot, make sure your sunscreen is waterproof.

Some products contain para-aminobenzoic acid, or PABA, used as a protectant, which can cause skin rashes in some people. Avoid products containing PABA. Other good protectants are titanium oxide and zinc oxide.

general

UV PROTECTION

- **All exposed body parts need protection equally.**
- **SPF-rated lip balms such as Chap Stick® are a good idea for these tender areas.**
- **Some sun protectants include moisturizers such as aloe vera that help the skin's healing ability, whether you're tan or not.**
- **Wear a hat to protect the scalp, and choose one with a long brim to protect the eyes.**
- **Don't forget sunglasses. Long exposure to the sun's rays contributes to cataracts. A cataract is the clouding of the vision due to thickening of the eye's liquid material. Ensure that sunglasses have both UVA and UVB protection.**
- **Sunblocks offer full protection from UVA and UVB, while sunscreens offer partial protection.**

if you get a
SUNBURN

- **A serious painful sunburn is often called sun poisoning.**
- **Antioxidant creams can promote healing of sunburned areas.**
- **Taking a daily multiple vitamin that contains zinc can promote healing of sunburn.**
- **Over-the-counter antibiotic creams can promote healing.**
- **Drink lots of water to encourage the body's healing.**
- **Light exercise or walking can promote healing by improving circulation.**

Oops! Ouch! Sunburn!

You're back from the beach, and your back, shoulders and feet are smarting. You skipped the sunscreen, and now you've got the first signs of a sunburn.

Sunburn is just that, a burn of the outer skin. It is more gradual than burns from fire, but there are three grades of sunburn, first, second and third degree, where first is the least severe and third is the most severe.

Each begins in the same way: The affected area feels hot quickly. For bad sunburns, this worsens over 24 hours.

A **first-degree** burn appears as irritated, lightly reddened skin, which is tender but otherwise looks normal. These burns usually improve by themselves. A simple moisturizer helps.

A **second-degree** burn is even redder, with some blistering, and painful to the touch. It may hurt too much to wear clothes, and the skin can be very dry. If the skin is intact, take a cold bath and apply ice to the most sensitive areas. Apply the ice for a few minutes, then remove, then reapply. This draws out the heat and halts further damage to deeper skin tissues. Apply over-the-counter cortisone creams or aloe vera sprays; reapply frequently. These ease the pain, soothe inflamed tissues and promote healing.

A **third-degree** burn appears worse. The skin may be wrinkled or darkened, have open sores or be numb in spots. *Do not use home remedies.* See your doctor immediately. In severe cases, skin grafts may be needed.

FROSTBITE AND FROZEN FEET

If you think of frostbite, you probably think of your feet first. Feet are more susceptible to frostbite than any other part of the body because they have the least blood circulation but the greatest exposure to the environment. Hands are a close second. Prolonged exposure to subzero temperature can cause skin to be damaged by another type of burn called freeze–burn or frostbite.

Any body part can suffer frostbite, but we will consider the feet. Cold usually affects the toes first. Pay attention, and if frostbite seems to be a threat, take immediate action.

some dos and don'ts

COLD DAMAGE

- **Multiple vitamins can speed recovery from cold damage.**
- **If a foot is frostbitten, cut the shoe off, do not pull it off.**
- **If socks are frozen to the skin, do not pull them off right away.**
- **After soaking the feet, apply moist heating pads.**
- **Mild exercise improves circulation and healing time.**

Common sense is the key to prevention. Use common sense. If you know you'll be in the cold, dress in layers. For the feet, that means double socks and waterproof shoes or boots. And remember, the longer the exposure, the greater the chances of cold damage.

Like sunburn, frostbite happens despite the best intentions, and this freeze-burn has three levels of severity.

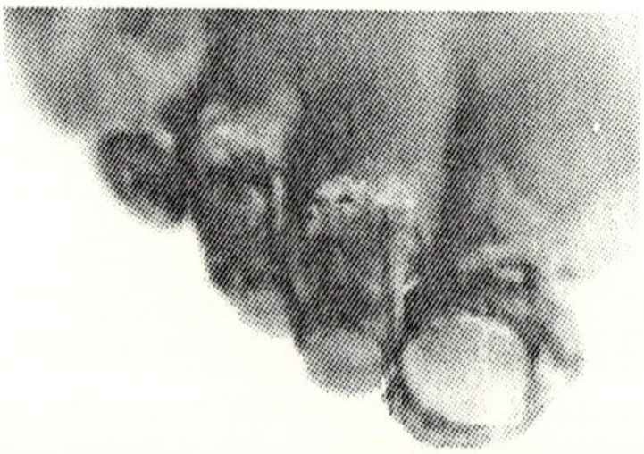

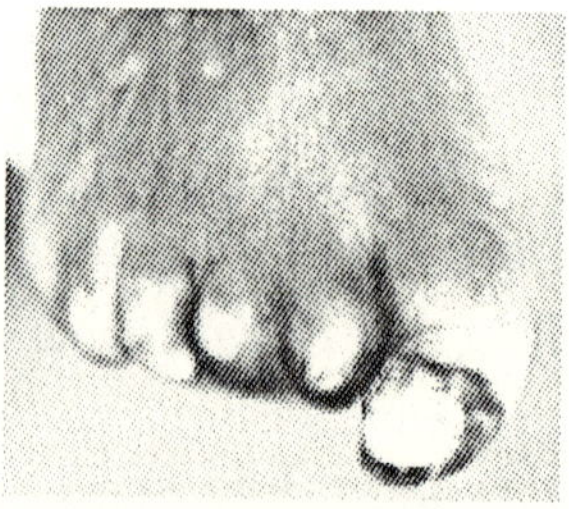

Advanced gangrene (left) of the toes caused by poor local circulation as with diabetes or by severe damage as a result of frostbite. The same foot (right) after irreparable damage by gangrene caused by frostbite and poor circulation. The tips of the small toes have fallen off spontaneously.

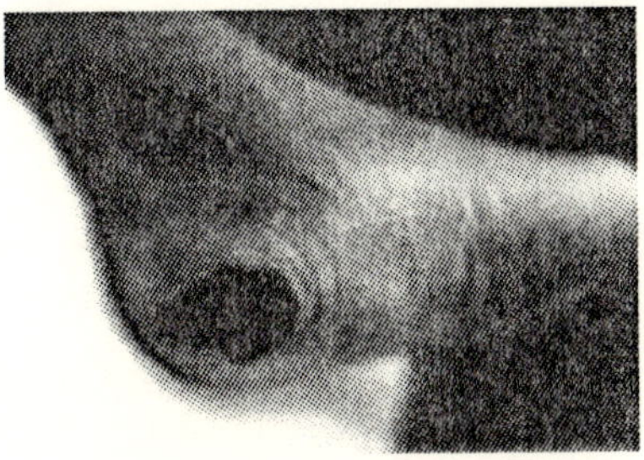

Another example of how gangrene spares no area of the feet. This is a large black area of the heel with severe gangrene that will undoubtedly require surgical amputation.

Stage 1, the least severe, involves loss of feeling but no real damage to the skin. Treatment involves gradual warming of the feet by going indoors. No special medication is needed.

In **Stage 2,** cold burn, the skin is damaged and is numb or tingly. It is partially frosted and has a whitish cast and feels hardened because circulation is diminished. To treat, slowly warm the foot, ensuring that the skin does not burn. Because of numbness, you may not know whether the water is too hot, so use lukewarm water only, testing with your hands. As feeling returns, increase the water temperature until it feels warm, but not hot. This will increase help circulation return to the affected area.

Stage 3, the worst case, is true frostbite, so called probably because the flesh actually freezes, so traumatically that it seems to take a bite out of the affected area. Freezing can cut circulation to zero, causing the affected tissue (sometimes including skin, muscles and bone) to die.

It is completely numb and turns black, becoming leathery and dry in appearance and touch. These are the telltale signs of gangrene, and immediate attention by a physician is required. Amputation of the blackened area is usually the outcome. Immediate response is crucial in saving the feet.

BEAUTY SALONS

While a manicure or pedicure can make you feel like you're in the lap of luxury, if you're not careful the treatment will have you in shock. Many nail disorders can spread from person to person. For instance, the nail fungus lives not only in the nail bed but also in the nail itself. When nails are trimmed by filing and cutting, bits of the nail remain on the file and clipper. If the instruments are used on the next person without having been cleaned, the bits of nail can come off and contaminate your nails with the fungus. Bacteria and viruses can be spread in a similar manner.

> beauty salon
> **CAUTIONS**
> - **Use only one beauty salon, and make sure you are familiar with its hygiene practices.**
> - **Fungi, bacteria and viruses can spread from unclean instruments to fingernails and toenails.**

To avoid this, you must ensure that the salon you select uses only sterilized or disposable instruments. A reputable salon will gladly demonstrate its sterilization process for you. Some salons use a special indicator that changes color when a sterilization procedure has been completed properly. Sterilized implements should be stored in dated containers, and if one has not been used in 90 days, it should be sterilized again.

Pay attention to the soaking fluids your salon uses. Insist on brand-new solution in a sterilized container. Rinsing is not sufficient. Containers—whether glass, stainless steel or ceramic—have pores or nicks that can harbor bacteria, fungi and viruses.

As long as the nail polish is new and not contaminated, nail polishing is fine, even if the nails are cracked, splitting or fungus-infected.

PHYSICAL EXAMINATION AND JOINTS OF THE FEET

A good physical examination—especially of the feet—is very important. No injury will heal properly if the feet are not healthy.

There are some tests you can do at home to check for the health of the bones of the feet. Start with joint movement, or *range of motion,* the distance a joint can move up and down and from side to side without pain or difficulty.

Here's what to do: Using your hands to help, move all your foot joints up and down and from side to side, checking to see whether they all are flexible and move without restriction. Move the ankle up and down; then the big toe up and down; the heel side to side; the front of the foot side to side; and all of the other toes by flexing and extending them. As long as there is no pain or clicking sounds while moving the joints, you then have sufficient range of motion.

Chapter 3

your feet and Circulation

Just as the heart needs to be in good condition for overall body health, circulation in the feet and lower extremities must be sound to maintain health and keep the area free of pain. This means that the connecting arteries (which deliver blood from the heart) and veins (which return blood to the heart) must be in perfect working order. To that end, self-examination can give you an indication of general foot health, and any problems that may be developing, allowing you to seek a professional's help early when problems do arise.

- **Raynaud's is a hereditary disease affecting circulation of the hands and feet.**
- **Taking a 50-mg niacin tablet every day can improve circulation of the body and feet and rarely has side effects.**

DIET AFFECTS CIRCULATION

Certain foods affect blood flow, and some can close blood vessels entirely, by affecting the tiny muscles that control them.

The most common substance that constricts blood vessels is caffeine, found in coffee, tea, cocoa and many soft drinks. Some headache medicines, such as Anacin, Extra Strength Excedrin, and the prescription drug Fiorinal, also contain caffeine. Long-term use of these products can be devastating to people with poor circulation, such as diabetics.

Check with your doctor or pharmacist to determine what is best for you.

Self-examination for Circulatory Health

The importance of good blood flow to the feet is perhaps best illustrated by discussing something that works against good blood flow: tobacco smoking. Smoking is the single most harmful action to your body's circulation. Diabetics, who are predisposed to compromised circulation, are especially vulnerable to increased problems due to smoking. Nicotine actually shrinks the blood vessels, reducing blood flow. This, then, reduces the blood supply along the arteries in the foot.

> - **Popping your knuckles can cause premature arthritis in the joints of the fingers and toes.**
> - **An injection of vitamin B_{12} can help improve cold and numbness in the feet and legs.**
> - **Taking vitamin B_1 orally can help improve circulation in the feet.**

Two main arteries supply blood to the foot, the *posterior tibial artery,* feeding the back of the foot, and the *dorsalis pedis artery* feeding the top of the foot. The capillaries of the toes take blood to the smaller places. So there are three main areas in which you can check for proper circulation in the feet.

You can take your *pulse* in your feet just like you can on your wrist. Here's how: Take the first two fingers and feel for a pulse back of the inner ankle and on top of the foot. If you can feel a pulse, then the main circulation is probably adequate. To check capillary circulation, press lightly on the end of each toe with your finger until the toe turns whitish, then release and see how long it takes for the natural skin color to return. This is the *capillary return time*. The normal capillary return time is 1 to 2 seconds; greater than 4 seconds is abnormal, and if there is any doubt, consult a health professional.

Other Circulatory Problems

If *varicose veins* are present, circulation in the legs and feet may be inadequate. A more subtle change may include dark spots all over the legs, front and back, which can range in size from tiny to rather large patches. The larger patches are usually lighter in color than the small spots and may be associated with aging in an elderly person. The patches, especially in the lower leg, may darken further and harden, becoming leathery. This is a preulcerative condition called *brawny induration*. Here the skin can break open and ulcerate to a deep infection. If this happens, a doctor should completely evaluate the situation. However, a good vitamin E oil or vitamin A cream can soothe and soften these spots. Apply it to the rough surface of the intact skin twice a day.

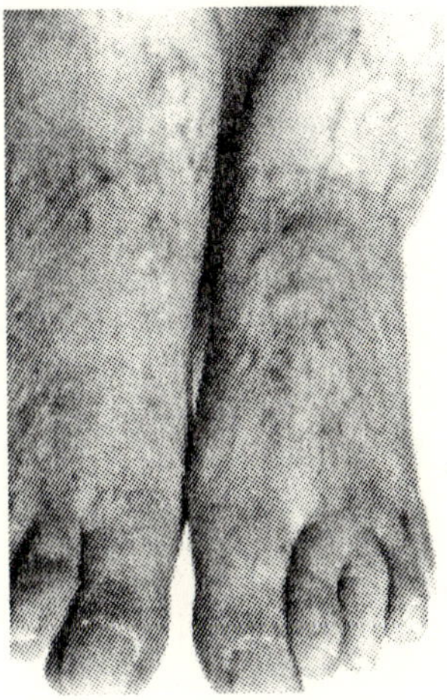

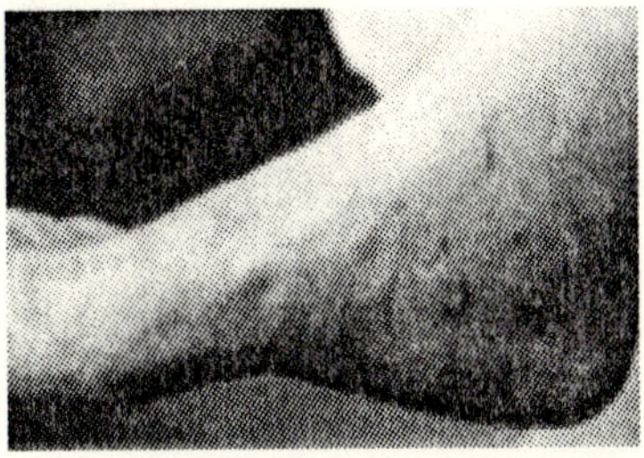

Varicose veins (left) are not uncommon to the feet and ankles and are a sign of poor blood vessel condition. The entire foot (right) may be enveloped by significant varicosities. They are especially common in diabetes and patients with debilitating circulatory conditions, such as hardening of the arteries (atherosclerosis).

The Most Unusual Legs

When a disease affecting circulation is traumatic, it can cause devastating effects on the skin over time. Such a disease is elephantiasis.

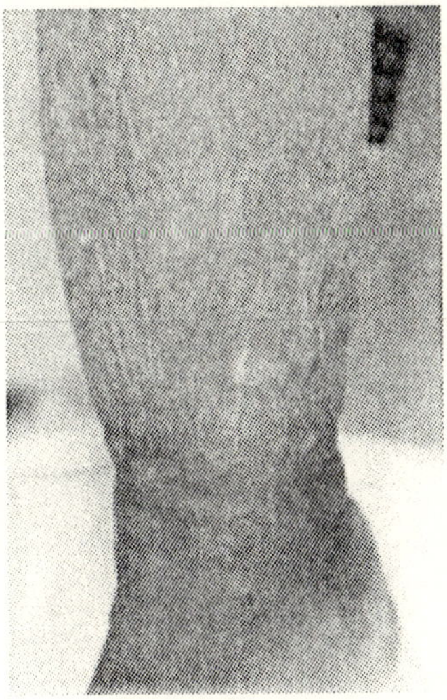

A leg and foot depicted with severe swelling. Note the leathery texture and irregular skin lines caused by problems with the lymphatic circulatory system sometimes a result of a filarial worm infestation.

STEPPING ON A NAIL

Unfortunately, it happens! You step on a nail, and it goes right through your shoe into the bottom of your foot. Aside from the obvious pain, you can take a number of steps at home to prepare and cleanse the wound to minimize pain and infection.

First, find the nail. Determine how long it is and how far it probably penetrated into your foot. Note any obvious contamination of the nail, such as dirt, rust, blood or other material. Try to determine if any part of the nail is missing and might have broken off inside your foot.

See a Pro

Within 24 to 48 hours, see a health professional for a *tetanus* shot or booster, especially if you have not had one within the past 5 to 10 years. This inoculation is to prevent tetanus, or *lockjaw,* a condition that is always fatal. The tetanus shot actually kills certain germs that infect puncture wounds, *anaerobic bacteria,* so called because they thrive without oxygen.

foot wounds

PUNCTURES

- **Never ignore a puncture wound of the foot.**
- **A tetanus shot will prevent lockjaw.**
- **Too frequent tetanus shots can reverse its effects.**
- **Most nail punctures cause little or no bleeding.**

Self-treatment

Keep the foot immobile, and keep all walking and standing to a minimum to prevent further trauma to the wound. To help cleanse and kill the anaerobic organisms, soak the foot in solution made of half warm water and half 3% *hydrogen peroxide,* which is available at most pharmacies and supermarkets. It is best to boil the water for 10 minutes to sterilize it, and then to let it cool before adding the hydrogen peroxide.

Soak the foot for 10 to 15 minutes. The hydrogen peroxide will release oxygen in the wound, so you may see some bubbling around the wound. This oxygenation helps kills the anaerobes. You may feel a slight burning sensation.

After soaking, apply an antiseptic such as Betadine in and around the wound. If you are allergic to iodine, use plain soap and water. Then apply an antibiotic ointment such as Bacitracin, Neosporin or Polysporin, and use a loose sterile gauze pad wrapped with rolled gauze to provide relief from the pressure of standing. (But keep standing to a minimum.)

It is important to assess the extent of the injury. Check to see if the foot and toes are moveable, especially in the area of the trauma. A nail that penetrates a joint can interfere with the movement of bones and can result in an infection of the bone or a bloodborne infection that will travel throughout the body.

SPRAINED ANKLE

At one time or another most of us have been hobbled by a sprained ankle. In a sprain, the ligaments and muscles of the ankle are stretched beyond their normal range, sometimes to the point of pulling away from the bones. The injury is accompanied by swelling and internal bleeding.

The first step in treating any sprain is to lie down very quickly and rest. To understand further treatment, it helps to understand the events that bring about the sprain and the symptoms.

What's a Sprain?

The body's natural protection against ankle sprains is to keep the muscles and bones of the ankle very close to one another, creating a locking effect. This prevents slipping or sliding of bones away from each other. This natural protection is removed when the foot is pointed downward, as when stepping off a curb or walking downhill, or when wearing high-heeled shoes. Such positions unlock the natural protection of the foot and ankle, allowing the foot to turn inward, and possibly resulting in an *inversion sprain*.

Sprains are classified into three categories depending on how much of the body's weight falls on this inward-turning foot and thus, the severity of the sprain. The injury will be worse if it occurs while running or playing sports such as skiing or rollerblading, where additional forces are at work on the ankle.

Three Degrees of Sprains

In a *Type I* (least damaging) ankle sprain, some weight can still be placed on the foot. Some minor swelling is visible, and the ankle bones, or *malleoli,* on either side can be seen prominently. The ankle and foot can be put through all movements without too much difficulty. Pressing on the skin will not create a lasting depression. Only the ankle is involved, and the foot is not affected.

In a *Type II* sprain, the ankle swells to a greater degree. The ankle bones are somewhat masked by the swelling, which is accompanied by redness and swelling of the entire ankle, extending to the foot. Slight weight can be placed on the foot. Although painful, the ankle can be moved in all directions. Pressing on the skin creates a depressed mark that will go away after a few seconds.

A Type *III* sprain is very painful. No weight can be placed on the foot, even for a short time. Swelling is complete, extending to the foot and the lower leg. Internal bleeding of the muscles is visible on the skin, as is bruising along the bottom of the foot. Movement of the foot is impossible because of the swelling and pain caused by *micro tears in the ligaments and muscles.* Pressing on the swollen skin creates a depression that may take as long as 60 seconds to disappear.

facts about
SPRAINS

- **A simple broken ankle is more easily treated than a severe sprain.**
- **Ankle sprains can be caused by worn shoes.**
- **The person with the worst-ever ankle sprain had to wear a leg and foot cast for three weeks.**

Is It Broken?

A Type III sprain can easily be confused with an ankle or foot fracture. In fact, if there is excessive bruising throughout the ankle and foot, it might well be a break, and a professional should be consulted. Fractures often are caused by severe sprains.

Try to identify the center of the pain by slightly pressing with your forefinger all areas of swelling to find the most tender spot. If a center cannot be found, it probably isn't a break, but a center of pain is usually the center of a break.

Treatment

Treatment of all three types of sprained ankles is basically the same, differing in the recovery time and the lingering of pain and swelling. For some Type III sprains not involving fractures, swelling can persist for more than a year.

The first thing to do, again, no matter how slight the sprain, is to get off the foot, stay off the foot, and apply cold, preferably ice, to the ankle. Place the ice in a clean towel; do not apply directly to the skin, which could cause an ice burn. *Do not soak* the foot or apply warmth to the injury: That will make it worse.

When you can, elevate the leg, ankle and foot, and for the first 72 hours, apply ice to the area for 20 minutes out of every hour.

Take a nonprescription medicine for pain and inflammation: ibuprofen, naproxen, ketoprofen, aspirin or acetaminophen—for the first week, around the clock, at the dosage given on the label. Ibuprofen or naproxen are recommended as first-line drugs. All except acetaminophen reduce both pain and inflammation; acetaminophen will reduce pain, but not inflammation.

People with bleeding disorders should avoid aspirin, which might promote additional bleeding. Take any of these medicines with food in order to minimize stomach discomfort. If you have a stomach ulcer, you should take only acetaminophen.

If the sprain does not improve even slightly in 24 hours, or if there is severe pinpoint pain in one spot, see a doctor, because the ankle may have been fractured. An X ray is needed, and if broken, the ankle will have to be put in a cast.

Assuming there has been some immediate improvement, yet if on Day 4 there is still pain or swelling, begin soaking. Twice a day, for 30 minutes each time, soak in warm water to which you have added 1 to 2 cups of Epsom salts.

Remember, a severe ankle sprain tears many of the muscles, as well as the tiny ligaments that hold the bones together and can take months or years to heal.

HEEL SPURS

A common foot-related complaint—especially in the city—is heel pain that turns out to be a symptom of *heel spurs.* A heel spur is a form of arthritis and inflammation of the soft tissues and muscles in one or both heels, usually caused by overuse of the foot—long-term standing on the job, or years spent walking on hard pavement in big cities.

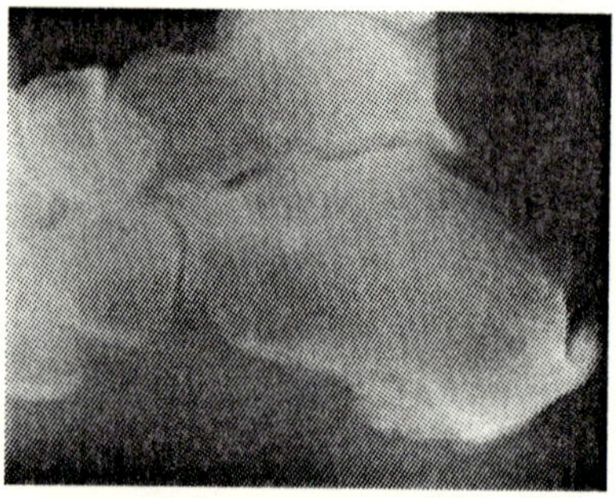

A prominent heel spur is shown in a side-view X ray of a foot. Note the ragged edges of the heel bone, referred to as spurring, located both on the bottom of and behind the heel.

Heel spurs usually form in one foot but can occur in both feet. The symptoms are sharp pain in the heel, most often in the morning upon getting out of bed. The pain also may occur after you have been sitting for a long time and then get up. The pain is sharp and travels up the leg along the nerve. First, you need to distinguish it from arthritis in the spine; if you have no arthritis in your back, you probably have a heel spur.

HEEL SPURS

- **Heel spurs are so common that one out of every four podiatry patents has them.**
- **A heel spur can be seen by X ray even when it has not caused symptoms.**
- **Anyone of any age can have symptoms of a heel spur.**

A heel spur is a buildup of calcium and fluid in the heel that causes local pain and swelling. This calcium is not related to diet or the amount of calcium consumed. Fluid buildup and swelling causes pressure on the muscle and nerve, resulting in pain in the heel when you stand up. The pain disappears after walking because you are not letting the fluid build up in the heel.

There are varying degrees of heel spurs. Some do not show up on X rays but have all the symptoms; the largest appear as large as the heel itself. Associated with heel spurs, a tightness of the muscles of the bottom of the foot, called *plantar fascitis*, can have similar symptoms.

The Ache of Plantar Fascitis

Tendonitis and plantar fascitis afflict many people, and overuse of the feet can irritate your the muscles and ligaments of the arches.

The plantar fascia, the anatomical name for the thin layer of muscle along the soles, can be overworked or injured in many ways, such as by running or jogging, being overweight, or repeated standing on the arches, as when climbing ladders.

Treatment is easily done at home. You're only dealing with sore muscles, so rest the feet, apply ice, or soak the feet in Epsom salts. All ease the muscular pains of the soles.

An elastic bandage can help; wrap it around the foot to cover the sole. So can stretching exercises for the sole and arch. These involve toe stepping, toe flexion and extension, rolling the arches on a special soft ball, and picking up a pencil or marbles with the toes.

Shoes, of course, play a key role, because they seat the bottoms of the feet. They should be well-cushioned, with insoles, and in good condition. Throw out shoes that are worn or tip to

warding off
PAIN

- **Don't wear the same pair of shoes two days in a row. This will help cushion the soles.**
- **Don't wear boots or pumps; they offer little support.**
- **Massage the soles daily.**
- **Pain relievers, such as ibuprofen, also relax the sole muscles.**
- **Use liniments on the soles if necessary.**
- **Walking barefoot on a sandy beach is excellent exercise for the plantar fascia.**
- **There are also two types of heel spurs, those on the bottom of the heel, and those at the back of the heel at the Achilles tendon. A person may have either or both types.**

one side; examine the wear patterns on the soles.

The Achilles Tendonitis Connection

The Achilles muscle attaches to the heel behind the ankle (posterior) and, like the plantar fascia, can also become tired. The Achilles (named for a Greek god who had a weak heel) is actually a group of muscles that terminate in the Achilles tendon, a long, skinny muscle that attaches to the heel. This tendon does most of the moving that involves the ankle.

It's easy to imagine the constant abuse inflicted on the Achilles muscle, especially when running or jumping. It holds most of the body's weight at the back of the leg. If it is not kept limber it can rupture or even become separated or partially tear away from the bones of the heel.

Overuse can create a spur in the region of the Achilles in the same way they form on the bottom of the heel area (see page 40) with the same symptoms of pain.

Overuse also can cause Achilles tendonitis, whose symptoms include pain, which is felt behind the heel when getting up from a chair or when moving after being inactive. Local pain and stiffness can be palpated behind the heel.

As the first line of treatment, for the first 48 hours, apply ice or cold to the heel. Elevate the leg with pillows and rest. After 48 hours, change to warm-water baths.

The next best treatment is to relax the muscle tendonitis and perform exercises targeted to help the muscles of the back of the legs and thighs (see page 58).

Changing shoes can also ease the pain. For women, heels help relax the Achilles by raising the heel higher. Men should wear spongy-soled heel inserts to lessen the blows to this posterior muscle from the foot hitting the ground while walking.

Home Remedies

Once you identify a problem as a heel spur, start treating them yourself. First, note that walking subjects your heels to forces equivalent to two to three times your body weight. Pad your heels to soften the pounding of walking. Several products for this purpose are sold in most drugstores and some supermarkets. Use a *doughnut pad,* so called because it has a hole in the center. The *heel cup,* similar to a doughnut pad but made of neoprene rubber and without the hole, has a built-in cushion that fits over your heel within your shoes. Another choice is the *orthotic* or *arch support* that is worn in the shoe. Incorporate the doughnut feature into the orthotic by cutting a hole in its heel area. An orthotic can be slipped in and out of whatever shoe you select and may be the most convenient solution.

foot health and
YOUR SHOES

- **The most comfortable shoes are made entirely of leather.**
- **The worst shoes—such as "jellies"—are made of plastic.**
- **The higher the heel, the more stress on the foot.**
- **Cheap shoes are never a bargain.**
- **The left foot is usually slightly larger than the right foot.**
- **Built-in insoles are a plus in shoes or sneakers.**
- **Wear high-heels only when necessary, and alternate with more comfortable styles, such as sneakers.**
- **A well-fitting shoe doesn't burn the skin; it's snug in front but not tight at the ball, tongue or heel.**

Try *soaking* the feet twice a day in a vibrating foot bath containing Epsom salts. Over-the-counter ibuprofen will help take away the inflammation and minor pain.

Wearing good shoes also helps. This means a soft wedge-type sole that does not have a separate heel. A strong *counter*—the panel behind the heel—and back side walls of the shoes also increase support of the ankle.

Foot Doc

Give self-care a few weeks. If you still have persistent pain, consult a doctor for closer analysis. He or she may recommend physical therapy.

A common treatment performed in the doctor's office is cortisone injections into the heel. Like ibuprofen, cortisone helps calm inflamed tissues. It also dissolves the spur to a slight extent. Despite rumors, these shots, done properly and in the right location, do not hurt more than a pinch and are not dangerous. The smaller the spur, as revealed by X ray, the easier it is to treat by injection alone rather than surgery. Treatment usually involves four injections two or three weeks apart.

Chapter 4

sensible
Shoes

It will come as no surprise that the most important single factor in foot health is wearing the proper shoe. Yet in many foot ailments the culprit is ill-fitting shoes, which can cause abnormal pressure on the feet, resulting in corns, calluses and ingrown toenails.

Your shoes should be comfortable from the first wearing. A good shoe should not have to be "broken in." The upper should be made of good, soft, genuine leather, with strong *counters,* or side walls at the heel.

At the toe, the shoe (this area is called the *toe box*) should be wide enough that the toes do not feel sidewise pressure. The shoe should have a soft sole and heel, preferably all one piece, as in the wedge-type sole, which distributes the pressure of the body's weight across the entire sole, instead of allowing it to concentrate in the heel.

Wearing stylish shoes or pumps is fine for short periods. But for longer periods, such as the work day, remove pumps or narrow stylish shoes whenever you can to allow the feet to rest. Wear sneakers ("tennis

FOOT WEAR

- **Don't wear other people's shoes; it can spread fungal infections of the skin and nails.**
- **Measure both feet when buying shoes, because they are not exactly alike.**
- **Nylon stockings in a closed shoe invite discomfort, because they trap sweat and odor.**
- **Open-backed shoes, or mules, are stylish but offer no Achilles support.**
- **Open-toed shoes expose the nails to dirt and fungus, so if you wear them, wash your feet at the end of the day.**
- **Orthopedic shoes offer the most support for special situations.**
- **Built-in insoles are a plus in shoes and sneakers.**

shoes") or wedge-type shoes at home and in your leisure time.

Shop for shoes early in the day to get the best fit. Feet tend to swell and would be at their widest in the afternoon or evening.

a shoe is a
SWEATBOX

- **Like the soles of the feet, the palms of the hands also have more sweat glands than the rest of the body.**
- **Spicy foods such as garlic and onions can increase sweating.**
- **To keep feet drier in summer, wear open-toed shoes or sandals.**
- **Keep a can of foot powder handy at work.**
- **Excessive sweating can invite fungal infection of the toenails.**
- **Use odor-neutralizing pads in the shoes, and change them regularly.**

Chapter 5

your feet and Lasers

The laser—the word stands for ***l***ight ***a***mplification by ***s***timulated ***e***mission of ***r***adiation—is effective in treating several foot conditions. A laser is a medical instrument that uses a special wavelength of light not visible to the human eye that is focused to become strong enough to vaporize skin or skin structures, somewhat like a magnifying glass can concentrate the sun's rays.

A key advantage to lasers is that they cause less pain, with less bleeding, and produce faster healing times than traditional treatments. One reason is that they do not destroy nerve cells but just sever them, so the cells can regrow quickly.

There are many types of lasers. The most common type used in the treatment of foot problems is the carbon dioxide laser, commonly known as the CO_2 laser.

LASERS

- **Can be used to reduce wrinkles.**
- **Are safe and emit safe levels of radiation.**
- **Do not work for and cannot be used for any bone surgery.**

In the treatment of foot problems, lasers are most often used to treat ingrown toenails, warts, parakeratosis and neuromas, or to make the initial incision for traditional surgery. The laser is trained on the affected area, where it penetrates the cells and causes the fluid to boil and evaporate in a plume of smoke. Lasers are not used on bone because they are not powerful enough and because bone doesn't contain enough water to allow vaporization.

Lasers, of course, must be used by professionals only. In the hands of the untrained, the instruments can be dangerous. Operators and patients must wear protective glasses.

Chapter 6

pinched
Nerves

If you have a sharp pain that shoots up the foot and toward the toes, chances are you have a *neuroma.* A neuroma (or more correctly, a *Morton's* neuroma) is a pinched nerve between the toes, in the middle of the foot. It usually can be traced to an injury—such as an object falling on the forefoot, or abnormal pressure from the wrong kind of shoes—that damaged a nerve.

You can check for a neuroma yourself. Squeeze your forefoot with a sidewise pressure. If you feel a shooting pain in the middle of the foot, it is probably a neuroma. If a different sort of pain results, consult a health professional.

Much of the pain of a neuroma is easily relieved. Wearing a soft-soled shoe takes pressure off the sensitive area.

on your
NERVES

- **Nerve damage feels like burning pain between the toes.**
- **Very ticklish feet indicate some sort of nerve abnormality.**
- **In the worst case of neuroma, the patient was crying from pain and not able to walk.**
- **Surgery for neuroma usually involves "blind" removal of the affected nerves.**

Exercising the foot will also help. Use the toes to pick up small objects, such as marbles. Or, extend the toes outward, spreading them at the same time.

You may also take a nonprescription anti-inflammatory drug, such as ibuprofen, naproxen or ketoprofen (Orudis). If these drugs cause stomach discomfort, have some nonprescription antacids on hand, such as cimetidine (Tagamet HB), famotidine (Pepcid AD), nizatidine (Axid), or ranitidine (Zantac).

Give this therapy a few weeks. If there is no change, consult a professional about cortisone injections, acupuncture or surgery.

Chapter 7

pedal support
Orthotics

Orthotics is an important approach to treating foot problems without resorting to surgery. Erroneously called arch supports, orthotic devices support the entire foot—toes, middle foot bones and heel. And they come in pairs, which serves to adjust both feet uniformly and adjust the body's entire posture.

For diabetics, orthotics can offset preulcerous conditions on the soles of the feet, preventing the formation of deep ulcers.

You can find the most basic type of orthotic at your pharmacy or supermarket, in the foot-care section. Such orthotics are great for the most common foot problems, such as fallen arches, minor calluses and corns, and minor back and hip pain resulting from foot problems.

More sophisticated orthotics, however, are required for more complicated problems, such as a short leg, heel spurs, bunions and hammertoe, or difficult cases of thickened skin on the soles. In these cases, see a health professional.

orthotic TIPS

- **Orthotics alone cannot preclude surgery.**
- **The manufacturer is as important as the material from which the orthotic is made.**
- **Orthotics must be adjusted periodically because the feet change.**
- **The most effective orthotic is usually not made of leather but of a composite of man–made materials.**

Chapter 8

the problems with
Bones

The human foot contains 26 bones. No wonder, then, that bones are the site of many types of foot conditions, with causes ranging from everyday wear and tear to genetics. Bunions may run in the family, but they are brought on more quickly from wearing shoes that are too tight, or from a career that keeps you on your feet for long periods.

> more on
> **BUNIONS**
>
> - **There are more than 150 ways to surgically correct a bunion.**
> - **A bunion on the little toe is called a bunionette, or Tailor's Bunion.**
> - **Most bunion surgery is done in the office.**
> - **Bunions and bunionettes can grow on the same foot at the same time, and on both feet.**

Bunions

Bunions, technically known as *hallux valgus* (or bowed big toe), are common and can form on either or both feet. A bunion is a growth of bone at the base of the big toe that protrudes on the inner side of the foot. Because there is little room for the extra bone in shoes, the tip of the big toe seems to bow inward toward the other toes of the foot. In doing so, it compresses the other toes together, causing corns between the toes, especially the two smallest toes.

Treat the corns using lamb's wool, as described on page 23.

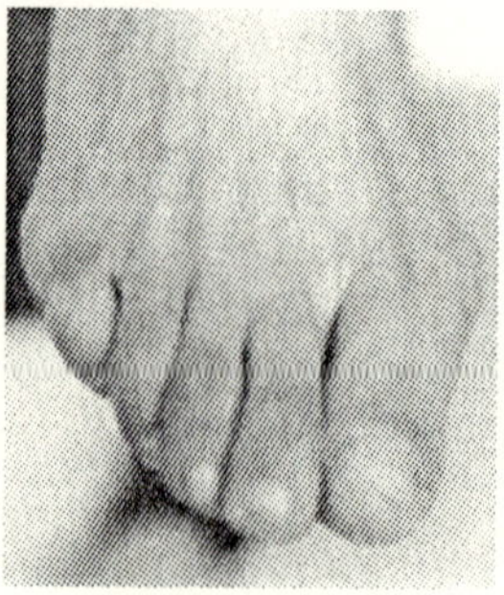

A significant bunion can be seen on the great toe joint area, and a small bunionette is visible on the little toe joint area.

Also, buy bigger shoes, with soft support on the bottom.

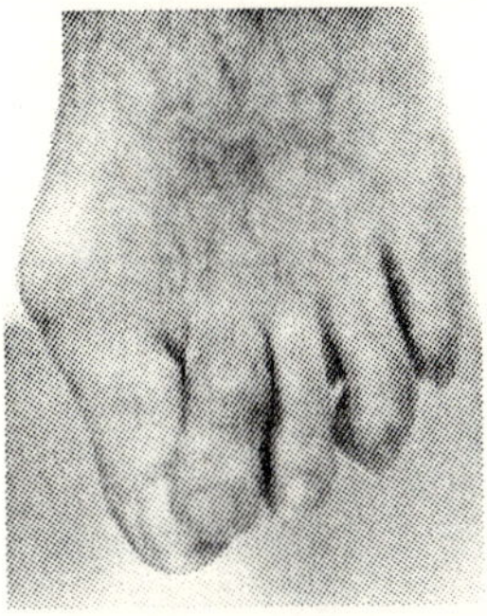

A classic bunion, with the outwardly bent big toe and overlapping second toe. Note also the corn on top of the second toe, which can become quite arthritic and painful.

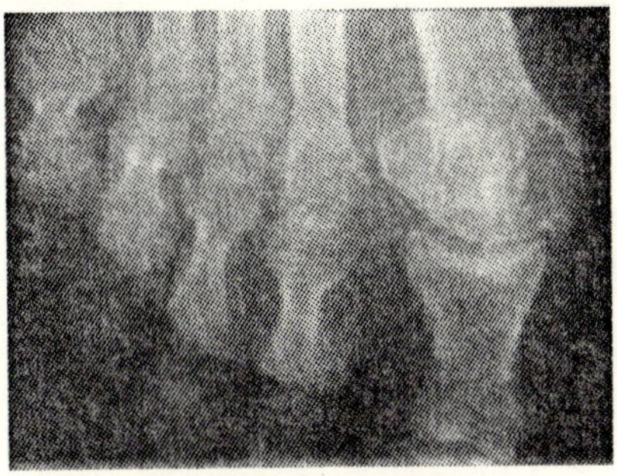

A top-view X ray of a foot showing a bunion (hallux valgus). Note the enlarged bone of the big toe causing a crooked first-toe section.

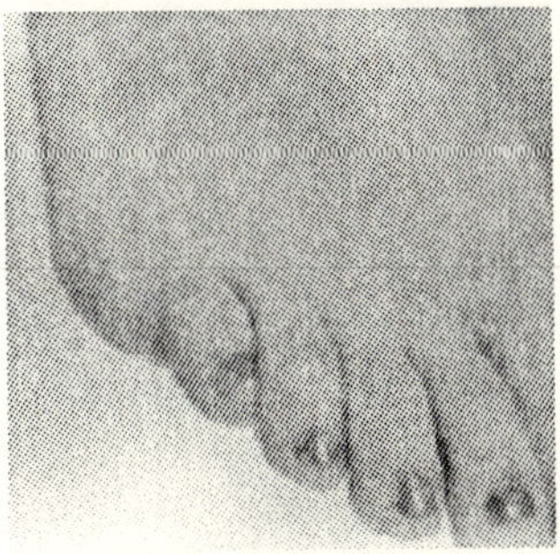

A large bunionette in the fifth-toe area, causing local pain and swelling that in a short time required surgical correction.

Hammertoe

Hammertoe is a common condition that can develop from bunions, although it also can develop independently. The cause is a gradual tightening of tendons in the sole of the foot.

Over months or even years, these dorsal or plantar tendons (the *extensor digitorum longus* and the *flexor digitorum longus*) tighten and contract. The two tendons oppose each other, and their contraction causes dorsal toe pain by cocking or hammering the toe at the interphalangeal joints. The hammertoe eventually can hit the top of the shoe, which is quite painful.

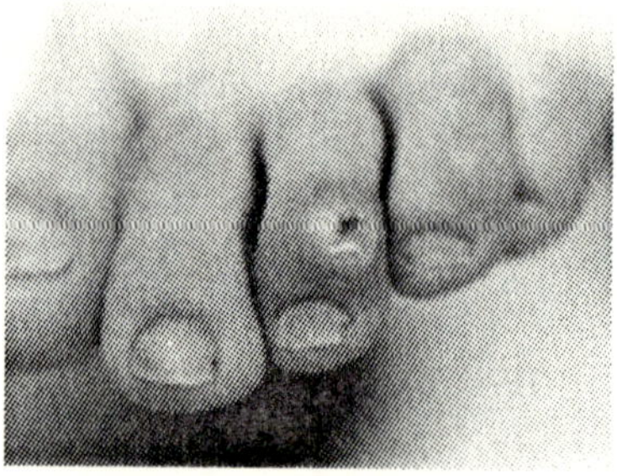

A typical surface corn formed by the flexed middle toe bone joints is called a hammertoe.

Many cases of hammertoe result from a bunion. The lack of room in the shoe causes the toes to curl up, or flex, increasing pressure on top of them. Again, corns can develop between the toes.

hammertoe
OUCH!

- **Hammertoe results from tiny muscle imbalances in the toes.**
- **Without treatment, they can progress to arthritis.**
- **Simple toe exercises can prevent symptoms.**
- **In the worst-known cases all the toes were locked in arthritis, and the patient couldn't walk.**

You can stop hammertoes from curling up and hurting by stretching the muscles along the bottom of the toes. First warm the toes in a bath, then use both hands to bend the toes backward and up. Be patient: This is a gradual process, taking three to six months. But it will help keep the toe muscles from tightening and the toes from curling, preventing the hammertoe from hitting the top of the shoe, and the pain that would accompany it.

For more serious cases, your doctor may consider surgery.

THE MYSTERY OF STRESS FRACTURES

It's every runner's nightmare: the stress fracture. It can come on suddenly and go away just as mysteriously. Also called a march fracture, a stress fracture occurs frequently in soldiers after a long march exercise, resulting from abnormal stress to a long bone (metatarsal) of the foot.

The most frequent is a hairline crack in the middle metatarsal bones, which can open slightly after strenuous exercise, causing localized pain. So, after jogging or other activity, if you feel pain in one area only, especially the top of the middle of the foot, you may have a stress fracture. Swelling is not

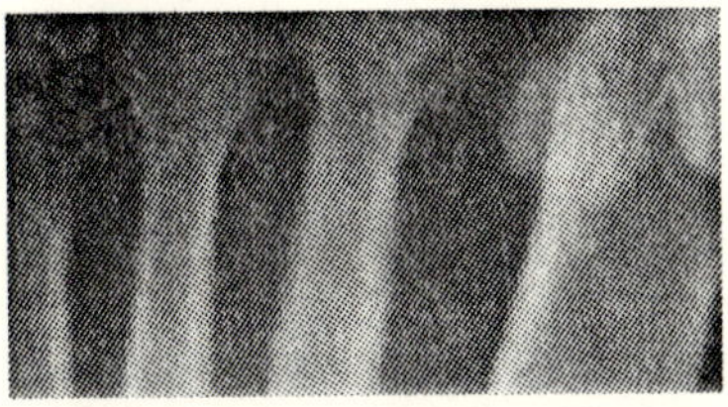

A top-view X ray of the foot depicts a difficult-to-recognize stress fracture. Note the center of the photo at the second metatarsal; the right border of the bone has a foglike edge, indicating a stress on the bone, confirmed by MRI.

always apparent or present.

Stress fractures occur only in the feet, usually arising from overuse of the middle bones and possibly from an injury to that area received when the foot was stepped on or while running on an uneven surface. This can cause a minor break in the bone's shaft and/or neck.

stress
FRACTURES

- **Stress fractures often affect only one foot**
- **Ibuprofen can lessen the pain.**
- **A lump can sometimes indicate the site of a stress fracture.**
- **Because of the inflammation, a stress fracture can be confused with a bone infection.**

Home treatment seeks to strengthen a weakened bone. Locate the area by feeling for the most sensitive point. Simply stop all stress and strenuous activity for a few weeks, and wrap the feet in a protective bandage, like a slip-on Ace elastic support. Also, place a soft insole in the shoes to protect the middle areas of the foot.

Nutritional approaches include vitamin D and calcium supplements, which help build bone mass in the affected foot.

If the pain has not abated in a few weeks, see a professional. He or she can examine the bones, identify the culprit using X rays, and possibly put the foot in a cast for a few weeks to promote complete healing.

Irritated Joints

When two bones constantly bump into each other or into the shoes, stress in the area develops into a soft mass. These sacs of joint fluid that sometimes hurt are called ganglions. They can occur anywhere on the bony surfaces of the body and at any age.

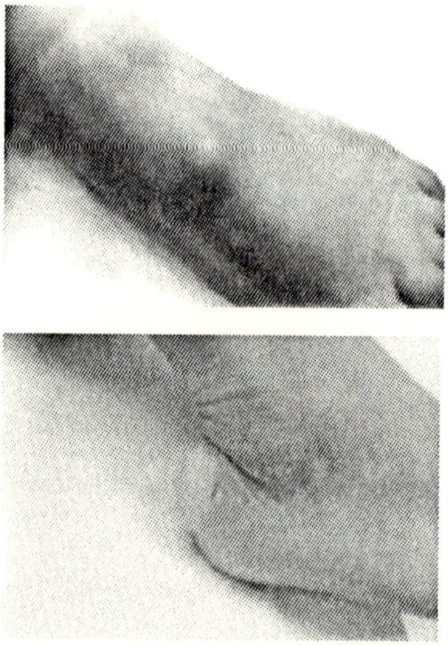

A ganglion (left, top) is a common spongy mass found in adults and children near bony joints. It is caused by repeated local trauma and is filled with leaking, jellylike joint fluid. It can be left untreated without consequence or drained by a doctor. A ganglion neglected for more than 20 years (left, bottom) develops an uncommon pathology. Note the large bulbous mass behind the heel that was painless until it caused the patient problems in finding a comfortable shoe; surgical excision was necessary.

Chapter 9

your feet are what you eat

Nutrition

Like the rest of your body, your feet need proper nourishment to function properly. First, you must follow a good, healthy diet. In addition, vitamins and nutritional supplements, including pills, creams and ointments, are available that are especially good for healthy feet.

Here are some basics. Follow the directions given on the container for proper doses.

> **feet and**
> **EATS**
>
> • **The body requires vitamins both inside and outside to heal properly.**
>
> • **The body's skin mirrors its nutrition.**
>
> • **The worst foot condition caused by poor nutrition involved large cracks on the heels and soles, and suprainfections.**

• **Multiple vitamin.** A good multivitamin with minerals is a great place to start for good basic foot health.

• **Gelatin capsules.** For brittle or cracking nails.

• **Antioxidants.** Try a formula that combines vitamins A, C and E, which are beneficial for proper skin and nail color and texture. For topical use, cut open the capsule and apply the liquid directly to the skin. On sore, rough spots, rub on a cream containing the same vitamins, as well as trace minerals.

• **Vitamin E cream.** This excellent supplement for the common condition of dry skin also comes in an oil form for direct penetration.

• **Royal jelly.** This substance produced by bees is an excellent adjunct to vitamin E for keeping the skin smooth. It comes in squeezable capsules that can be cut open for direct application to any skin surface.

• **Inositol.** A B-complex vitamin. Take 2 grams per day to help increase circulation in the feet and legs.

• **Cocoa butter.** This natural lubricant is great for keeping the skin of the feet soft and supple.

For difficult conditions, your doctor can prescribe special creams and ointments, such as:

• **Retin-A.** This good topical agent is a concentrated vitamin A mixture that is excellent for dry skin. However, overuse can make the skin drier. Never use it in strong sunlight, which can cause a severe rash.

Remember the main difference between creams and ointments. An ointment is oil-based, and a cream is water-based. The oily ointment is best used on dry skin that is cracked—to prevent further cracking. Creams are better for normal, intact skin.

• **Renova** This prescription cream can also help repair damaged skin. Although it contains tretinoin, the same active ingredient as Retin-A, it also moisturizes the skin, whereas Retin-A is drying.

Also classified as a vitamin A cream, Renova can reduce fine wrinkles by moisturizing the skin. It penetrates more deeply than any over-the-counter cosmetic creams containing alpha-hydroxy acids, which only remove superficial dead skin cells.

For optimal results, use Renova daily for three to six months. Remember to avoid direct sunlight when using the cream, or redness, drying and peeling may result.

Chapter 10

workouts and feet
Sports

With the level of popularity exercising has reached in the millennium, as part of the trend toward better health, sports medicine of the feet deserves our attention.

Each sport is different in terms of the forces exerted on the feet. Walking or jogging produces forward motion. Tennis, basketball and volleyball require more side-to-side motion. And ice-skating, roller-blading and in-line skating result in a combination of forward and side-to-side motions.

For a side-to-side sport, the shoe should provide extra ankle support and have a stiffer counter. A forward-motion sport needs a shoe with more support and stiffness in the toe box.

A combination sport, such as in-line skating, requires coordination of feet, ankles and legs and proper balancing of the entire body. These sports can be dangerous if not done properly. The correct in-line skate needs the qualities of a good shoe and must provide high ankle support for good leg control. The heel area should be deep enough to seat the heel snugly and minimize forward and backward motion of the foot. The sides of the back should be strong enough to support side-to-side motion without bending excessively. Check this by flexing this part of the skate before you buy it.

A sure sign that the skates do not fit properly is a pain that develops in the shins after a period of use. If you experience pain and swelling in this area, you probably have *shin splints,* which are stressed muscles in the shins. Shin splints require rest and elevation of the legs.

Your footwear is the most important part of maintaining healthy feet, and using proper footwear is especially important in sports shoes. Even for skates, follow the advice in Chapter 4 for selecting good shoes. Following these guidelines, you will have excellent support and healthy feet all your life.

For the greatest safety, buy the special add-on supplies for your sport, such as wrist, elbow and knee protectors and helmets.

Exercising the Feet (and the Body)

Exercising is as important for the feet as for the body overall.

Good health means keeping top-notch muscle tone all over. Generally, taking a brisk walk three times a week for 20 minutes is all you need to maintain great skin color and good circulation in the lower extremities.

For a specific foot problem, you'll target specific muscles, and that requires a little knowledge of anatomy. Before any exercise therapy, soak the area in warm water for at least 10 minutes to prepare the muscle for training. If you're over 50, check with your doctor before you begin any strenuous exercise.

Tight Muscles: Soles and legs. To help a heel spur, which is a muscle imbalance in the sole, you will want to stretch the muscles of the soles (plantar fasciitis) and the Achilles tendon behind the heel.

First, extend the forefoot, stretching the toes up and out. Then flex the toes tightly all the way in, like a fist. Repeat this cycle. This will activate the arch and sole muscles that extend to the heel. You know when you are doing this correctly when you feel tightness in the soles. Next, use all the toes to pick up a pencil, activating the toe and sole muscles. Finally, gently massage the foot by rolling the arch over a soft object while putting some of your weight on the foot. Special balls are sold for this purpose. Do these exercises for 10 minutes each night, after a warm bath or shower.

Another exercise for the soles is the leg stretch. Lean into a table, chair or wall and point both feet straight ahead and parallel to each other. Then move one leg behind the other; the rear leg is the one to be stretched. The farther back the leg, the greater the stretch. Lean into the stretch and move gently back and forth, steadily and slowly, for about 10 minutes. If you are doing the stretch properly, you will feel the stretch in the bottom calf muscle, or gastrocnemius, and the Achilles tendon. Again, do this stretch in the evening after a warm shower.

A third exercise involves rising up on your toes, taking care that your weight is distributed evenly over both feet. This is a good overall exercise for the main muscles in the top and bottom of the foot, as well as the ankle muscles. Do it every day for 10 minutes.

For stretching the inner thighs, hamstrings and calf muscles, kneel down, with your toes and feet pointed backwards and your shins along the floor, and sit back on your ankles. If too much muscle tightness is felt between the thighs, proceed slowly. This exercise is excellent for stretching the inner thighs—the hamstring muscle group—and calf muscles.

Sports. The feet do not work alone but in unison with the rest of the body. Sports, for young and old, require a limber and well-maintained muscle system. Before you get out there and start moving around, do a few easy exercises to warm up.

> **SPORTS**
>
> - **The body requires warmup for all activities.**
> - **You must set yourself a limit in sports.**
> - **Athletic footwear supports the whole body, not just the feet.**

- Bend sideways into one knee with the other leg outstretched behind you, then alternate until you feel tightness in the calf muscles.
- Hold the right ankle with the right hand. Pull the leg up while bending the knee until the foot reaches the buttock or until you feel tightness in the leg. Alternate, and repeat several times.
- Isometrics is an ideal way to tone up all types of muscles. It's a resistance-type workout in which you can flex and extend all joints by either tightening them in place or pressing them against a stationary object. The purpose is to stimulate the nerves and muscles, getting them ready to fire when needed.

This is just an overview of how to warm up. Just remember that preparing for sports is just as important as playing the sport itself. A stiff body is dangerous and could result in muscle tears and broken bones.

Chapter 11

for those with Diabetes

Much of the advice in this book does not apply to diabetics. A diabetic must consult a podiatrist or other foot specialist before attempting any kind of self-treatment of foot ailments. For diabetics, what seems a minor foot problem could have dire consequences.

In diabetes, which can begin in childhood and adulthood, the body does not produce the hormone insulin. Without insulin, the body cannot properly use glucose, a blood sugar. Other problems can develop, such as blindness and poor circulation in the feet. Diabetes is a long-term disease and must be properly diagnosed and treated by a doctor.

special tips for
DIABETICS

- **Poor diet and uncontrolled diabetes can cause burning and numbness and discoloration of the feet and nails.**
- **Ticklish feet are not funny for a diabetic—they are usually a sign of underlying nerve problems if you already have diabetes.**
- **Foot infections spread like wildfire in diabetics and are usually caused by more than one organism.**
- **Diabetics usually have major foot problems within 20 years after diabetes has been diagnosed.**

Because of long-term complications such as poor circulation, diabetes

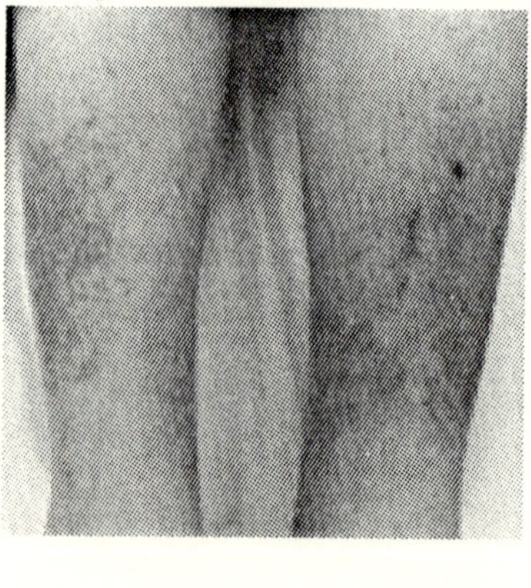

Mottling of skin of the legs is a sure sign of poor circulation and leaking blood vessels commonly afflicting diabetic patients.

c. . lead to numbness and possible amputation of the feet due to *osteomyletitis,* an infection of the bones. Symptoms of poor circulation include pins and needles, a tingling sensation, cold feet, calf cramps (especially at night), and a burning sensation on the plantar surface.

Obviously, diabetics should be especially careful when examining and

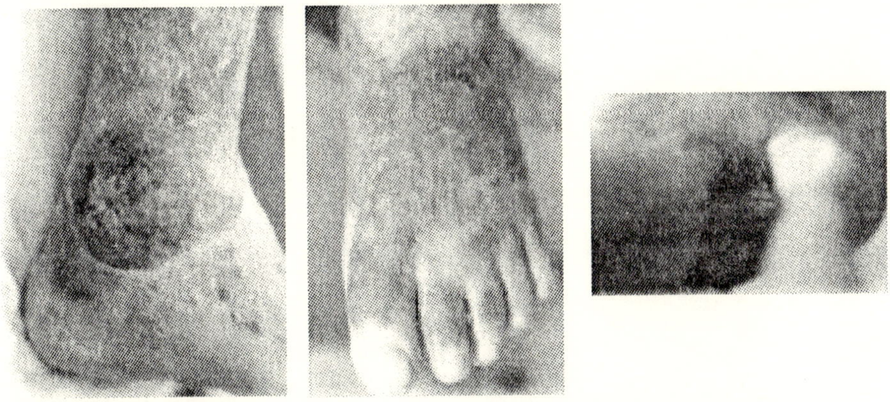

Severe diabetic ulcer (break in skin, far left) in ankle and leg, associated with poor skin tone and poor local blood flow. The cardinal signs (center) of poor circulation caused by diabetes. This foot has the appearance of surface discoloration indicative of severe internal blood vessel damage. Interdigital maceration (right) between the toes can be the start of a severe infection leading to gangrene and amputation.

caring for their feet. Here are a few tips for continued good foot health:

- Don't walk barefooted.
- Don't smoke. It constricts blood vessels and impairs circulation.
- Cut toenails straight across and don't dig in the corners.
- Wash the feet daily; inspect and carefully dry between the toes. In diabetics, interdigital maceration (wetness) and infection between the toes are common because the sweat, which contains sugar that was not used by the body. This causes a breakdown of the skin.
- Check the feet and ankles for changes in color (darkening or lightening) or in texture (peeling skin and calluses or corns). Any change may indicate a preulcer condition, in which the skin is near breakdown, which diabetics might not sense due to numbness.

• Avoid open-toe and thong-type shoes that may expose the feet to trauma by excessive rubbing.

• For temporarily relieving burning sensations in the soles, over-the-counter creams such as Zostrix HP and Capzasin Plus are effective. They contain a natural extract of cayenne pepper.

Chapter 12

the unforgettable feet of

Babies and Infants

Babies and infants also suffer from foot problems, sometimes from birth. The feet of newborns are always examined by a professional, but you can always perform your own foot exam for your baby.

Look over the baby's whole body. Check the skin color and hue. It should be of uniform texture and show no unusual discoloration or spots. Look along the legs and check that the hips, knees and feet are equally spaced on both sides and are symmetrical.

Look more closely. Place the knees equally forward and look at the feet. They should be equally pointed in similar directions. The arches should be equally flat. Move the toes and feet from side to side. The feet are pliable and the joints and bones should move easily in all directions.

> in baby's
> **BOOTIES**
>
> - **All babies are born with flat feet and are bowlegged.**
> - **All babies are born with intoe (feet pointing inward).**
> - **Babies' bones are like gelatin for the first year.**
> - **Late-term babies are especially prone to club foot.**
> - **A baby can have a dislocated hip unbeknownst to either of you.**
> - **Wearing shoes on the opposite feet can sometimes correct mild metatarsus adductus.**

Look closely at the toes. Do they seem to be stuck together? This condition, syndactyly, is common and normal. Check the toe movements, ensuring that they flex and extend and looking to see whether a toe overlaps another. This is rare, and when it happens usually affects one foot only.

Treat overlapping toes yourself. Soak the foot in warm water, then exercise the toes in the opposite direction from the overlap position. Tape the toe

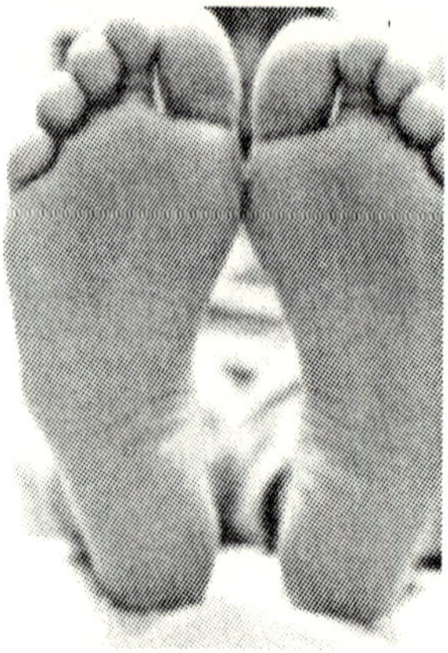

Metatarsus adductus in a child's foot. Note the exaggerated inward curve of the forefoot starting at the outer bump midway down the foot, a congenital deformity requiring treatment using "straight-last" shoes and corrective plaster casts.

to neighboring toes to hold the position. Continue this for several weeks to several months, depending on progress. If even slight results are not seen in a few weeks, see a professional, who may X-ray the foot to examine its bone structure.

Next, look at the fronts of the feet and compare them to the heels, evaluating the alignment of the forefoot. A marked inward bend only at the front of the foot may indicate a birth defect called metatarsus adductus, part of a club foot problem that a doctor will use splints to correct.

To check for hip dislocation, place the index finger of each hand into each side of the baby's hips and compare where they are in relation to the legs. They should be exactly opposite each other and not distant up or down and apart from each other.

Chapter 13

children's Growing Pains

From the foot's perspective, childhood is defined as the period from age 2 to age 7. Children's bones grow rapidly, filling with calcium and maturing to support extra weight, and walking patterns develop.

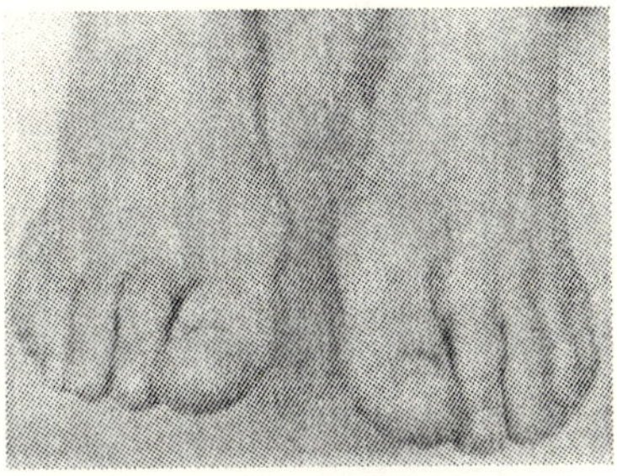

An example of premature growth of bunions in both feet of a 12-year-old child. Children are not immune from developing adult-onset bone deformities, which require corrective surgery at age 18.

The first step—literally—is the transition to upright mobility. Never compel a child to start walking, but let him or her gradually get used to standing briefly and falling back until upright all the time. Forcing a child to stand up prematurely can cause excess strain on the body and even injure muscles and joints. Allow 12 to 15 months for a child to walk completely upright. Meanwhile, the use of a walker can allow the body to get used to using the feet and legs, gradually strengthening the muscles.

- **Children should not pick their nails; it can invite fungal infection.**
- **Children should exercise their toes with their hands for proper mobility.**

Don't consider shoes for walking until your child is walking. Until then, a roomy, soft baby shoe or sneaker can protect the feet. Choose leather for proper breathing of the feet, but provide enough warmth, because a child's feet are especially susceptible to cold. Never be critical of the child's first steps. He or she is learning and will continue to learn for six more years.

A good walking shoe is roomy all around the feet. The material must be breathable but closed, and the sole and heel must be supportive. When shopping, bend the shoe from front to back. It should be resilient and return to its original shape, but still be flexible. This will allow support without strain.

Once the child begins walking regularly in shoes or sneakers, evaluate his or her whole body movement during walking and, as the child develops, during running and sports activity.

Be alert for warning signs: taking the shoes off frequently, complaints of painful shoes, tired feet. The problem may be shoes that are too small, too much activity at once, poor arch support, or leg problems, such as bowlegs or knock-knees.

Take off the shoes and socks and examine the feet for excessive sweating. Look for signs of friction where shoes may be too tight; check for reddened areas or rashlike spots, and don't forget the sides of the feet. This could indicate tight shoes. Examine the shoes, especially the soles and heels. On each shoe, signs of wear should be even on both sides. Uneven wear could indicate that one leg is shorter than the other, or is turned inward or outward more degree than the other.

If there is no severe intoe or outtoe, the child will probably grow out of minor bowleggedness or knock-knees. But be alert if the child does not develop a good

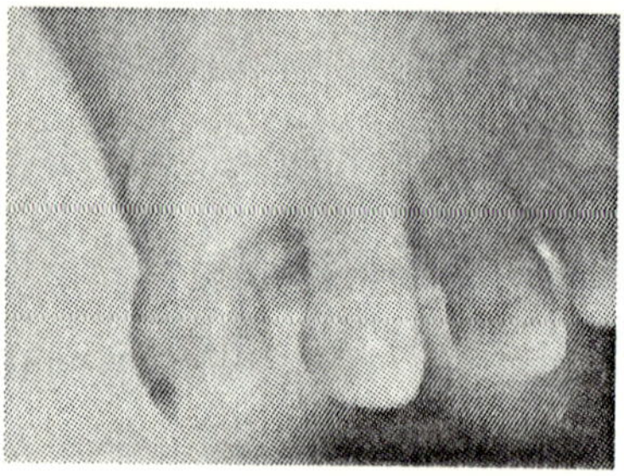

A small ganglion on the little toe of a child. This enlarged area was formed as a result of an uncorrected toe walking gait, creating excessive pressure between the toes.

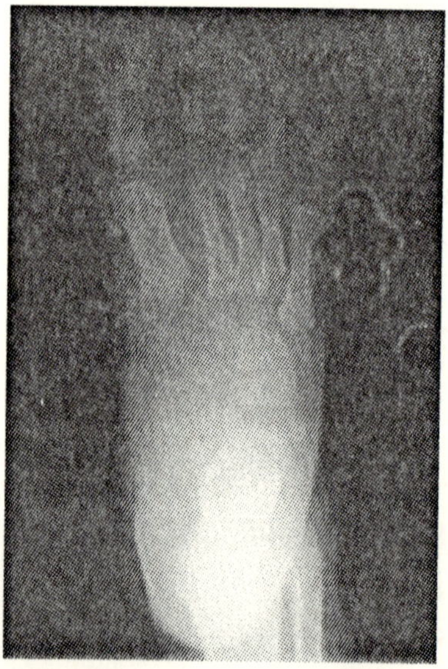

A top-view X ray of a child's foot. Note the absence of many bones. Babies are born with soft cartilage not seen in X rays, and this cartilage converts slowly to bone during childhood.

running and walking cycle. In cases of constant tripping and falling and frequent feelings of fatigue, consult a professional. These conditions could result in club foot or toe walking, which are major problems in the development of foot muscles and may need corrective surgery or targeted exercises.

A child may often complain of leg, foot or ankle pains that come and go with no pattern. These are the classic growing pains that are usually correctly dismissed as normal. However, always examine the shoes and feet before reaching that conclusion. If any sign of a problem is detected, consult a professional.

Usually a good soaking bath of the entire body and a gentle massage of the affected area work wonders for growing pains. The culprit is usually tired muscles that have been overactive, or worn-out shoes that should be replaced.

Chapter 14

a royal pain

Gout (Podagra)

Gout was once considered a rich man's disease because it was thought to be caused by rich foods and alcohol. In fact, diet is implicated, and dietary changes are part of the treatment. It used to be thought of as a disease of royalty because of the rich diets of kings and queens.

It has even been confused with another disease called pseudogout, which mimics its symptoms. In either case, the foot is the first part of the body to be affected.

Gout is an accumulation of uric acid in the joints, especially in that of the big toe. It is therefore most confused with bunions and bunion pain. Uric acid forms crystals that are shaped like tiny sewing needles. These crystals clog the joints and cause severe pain when the bones try to move against each other. Redness and swelling also can result, and the foot feels hot and throbs endlessly.

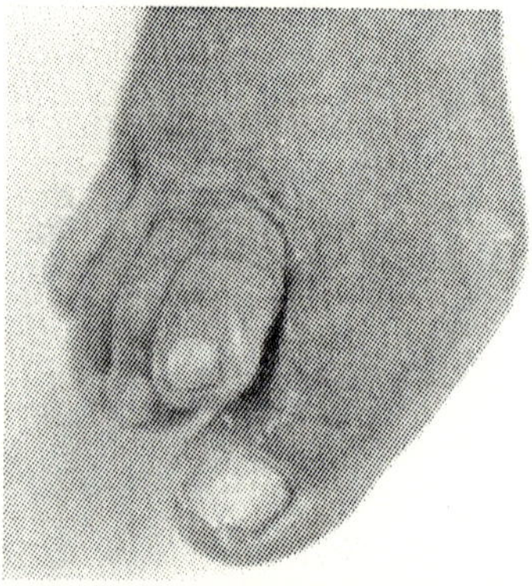

An area of chronic gout seen at the great toe joint. This is where the first signs of gout appear. Note the severe local swelling, accompanied by redness and stiffness of the forefoot.

Treatment

At least identify the symptoms so you can be prepared if you need to see a doctor. The onset of gout is slow, as the uric acid deposits in the joint take time to build up. The pain will come and go until it eventually becomes very painful. It is common to get acute big toe painful attacks over many years.

Apply ice to the painful area off and on for each hour, and elevate the feet to reduce swelling. Do not soak in warm or hot water, because heat

about
GOUT

- **Place a bag of crushed ice or frozen peas over the foot to relieve pain and inflammation.**
- **Gout usually affects only one foot at a time.**
- **Gout is a form of arthritis.**
- **Gout is hereditary.**
- **Gout can occur anywhere in the body.**
- **A sac of accumulated uric acid is called a *tophus*.**

worsens the pain.

Watch your diet, to cut down on foods that promote the formation of uric acid in the system, including legume-type beans, organ meats, red meat and alcoholic beverages. Drink plenty of water to increase the amount of uric acid that is excreted in the urine. Lose weight if necessary to ease the pressure on the feet. Find comfortable shoes and soft insoles to lessen the pain and the swelling of the big toe and joint.

If no relief is found after a few weeks, see a professional, who will diagnose gout by examination, a blood test for uric acid levels, and a test of the joint fluid for uric acid crystals.

The doctor can prescribe medicine for the acute attacks of gout pain and to lower uric acid levels in the blood. The process is slow, so be patient. It may take a year to lower uric acid levels enough to stop gout.

Chapter 15

your bones and Arthritis

If you haven't had arthritis in some form, chances are you know someone who has.

There are two types, rheumatoid arthritis (RA) and osteoarthritis (OA).

Rheumatoid arthritis, which is genetic, involves the joints of the entire body, including the feet. In the feet it advances especially to the toes and can cause a debilitating limitation of motion in the joints.

Rheumatoid arthritis is an autoimmune response, for an unknown reason, in which the body's immune system attacks the bones. The joints and spaces in them become narrow and clogged with calcium, the same material of which bones are made; joints feel like sandpaper or may stop moving entirely. In the feet, this may be most noticeable in the little toe, where the joints can fuse together and become immobile. There is no cure for the condition, but, in general, exercising all joints can prolong the bones' movability.

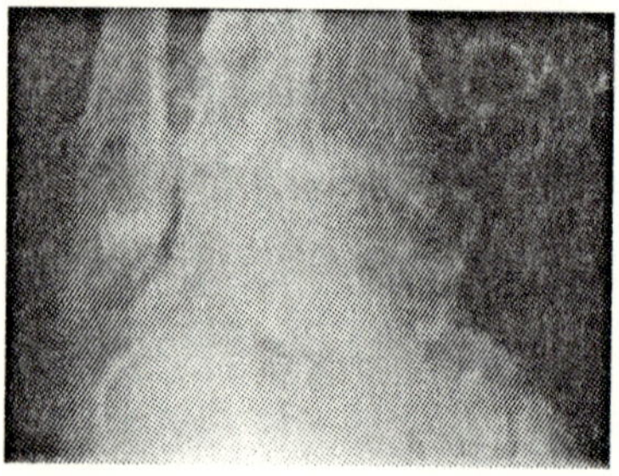

A front-view X ray of an ankle joint afflicted with arthritis. Note that the joint lines between bones are not smooth but instead have become jagged and irregular filled with calcium deposits limiting their movement. This process is rheumatoid arthritis.

Osteoarthritis is a different matter and involves conditions that are the opposite of those of rheumatoid arthritis. In osteoarthritis, calcium is depleted from the bones through the blood and urine, and excreted, rendering the bones thin and brittle. A main cause is thought to be hormonal changes in postmenopausal women and in older men over age 60.

Thinning of the bones can cause premature bone fractures without warning, especially at the hip joints. The feet are also of concern because they are so important in supporting the body's weight.

The best way to alleviate the problems associated with low calcium is to rebuild body stores by daily exercise and calcium supplements. Take one pill daily of 500 mg calcium combined with vitamin D, such as Os-Cal or Calcitrate.

Other supplements and herbal preparations can also help. Some that relieve the inflammation of arthritis without a prescription include shark cartilage (500-mg capsules), the hormone DHEA (25-mg tablets) and the herb cat's claw.

A recent discovery that actually reverses arthritis is a complex of glucosamine and chondroitin with vitamin C and manganese. Glucosamine is a nutrient found in most all foods in small quantities and in our bodies, and chondroitin is a substance like a kind of fatty tissue found in most animal products. Together, in the proper quantities, they help replenish cartilage in injured joints by stimulating production of new cartilage and reduce the action of enzymes that can harm the joint lining. This helps reconstruct the joint's original soft cartilage lining and the connective tissue needed for proper movement of bones. Dosage depends on body weight but ranges from 1,000 mg to 2,000 mg of each daily. The better formulas include vitamin C for better absorption of the complex and manganese, an essential building block for maintenance of solid bones. It is, however, controversial whether to use the sulfate form of the complex and is thought to be beneficial because of the role it plays in building up basic cell health.

more about

ARTHRITIS

- **Even the walls of arteries can become stiffened with calcium deposits**
- **Rheumatism is another name for rheumatoid arthritis.**
- **Taking calcium-fortified Tums® will help build bones.**
- **Drinking milk or taking yogurt daily can help build up calcium in the body.**

DHEA—dehydroepiandrosterone—is a hormone manufactured by the body. It is a basic hormone that makes up a generic pool for the body to use when needed. Supplements can help in stressful episodes of low hormone levels.

Chapter 16

your feet and Pregnancy

Being pregnant and having a baby are wonderful--but not for your feet, as anyone who has been pregnant can attest.

In general, the feet become swollen and painful as pregnancy progresses. This is due to the greater physical shock with every step as body gets heavier. This increases geometrically when a pregnant woman walks or runs. Moderate, gentler exercise is better, if you feel well enough, such as low-impact aerobics, calisthenics, walking and slow jogging.

If you are unlucky enough to be pregnant in summer, your feet may swell even more. And pregnancy causes water retention (edema), as well as high blood pressure (hypertension). Both can increase pain in the feet.

But don't worry, the body is resilient, and after your baby is born, you'll have happy feet again.

> special tips for
> **MOMS TO BE**
>
> - **Elevate the feet higher than the heart several times a day to decrease swelling.**
> - **Wear open shoes in summer to allow for swelling.**
> - **Massage the feet to decrease swelling and pain.**
> - **Extra-wide sneakers are the most comfortable shoes. Don't wear heels.**
> - **Do not wear nylon stockings; they can restrict circulation in the legs.**

To minimize the pain of swelling feet during pregnancy, wear insoles and extra padding in your shoes as needed. You can buy them at any drugstore, and they are made of moleskin, foam and other soft manmade materials.

Soak your feet in warm Epsom salts baths. This can help draw out local swelling. Apply moisturizers and vitamin-fortified creams and lotions, such as vitamin E, which can help skin that has dried or cracked because of the temporary hormonal changes during pregnancy.

Chapter 17

your health in Walking

The importance of walking for the general health cannot be overstated. A regular walking regimen benefits the body by building up the immune system, improving mood (including a better sex life), combating depression by getting you out of the house, helping you lose weight, reducing constipation, improving circulation, and warding off arthritis by keeping the joints mobile and building up calcium in the bones.

Anyone who has been inactive for any time, including a temporary illness affecting the feet, can testify to the importance of regular walking. Without regular exercise muscle tone is lost, and pain sets in because, when exercise is resumed, muscles swell, closing up joints. A person in a wheelchair thus can notice the swelling of the calves and feet with associated excruciating pain when trying to move the limbs.

Contractions of the calf muscles during walking functions as a pump that helps the heart move blood to and from the legs. Exercising these muscles provides a tremendous boost to the tissues in the lower legs and feet, which always need the constant flow of nutrition from the blood.

Walking is a great exercise during pregnancy, if the woman feels up to it. Diabetics and people with even borderline high blood pressure can improve their conditions with a regular walking cycle. Walking is good for a person who may be predisposed to colon cancer, because it promotes digestion and excretion, speeding the elimination of fats and toxins and indirectly reducing cholesterol. Walking increases the body's metabolism, burning more calories and encouraging weight loss.

Treat regular walking with respect. Consider your age before undertaking an exercise program, especially if you're over 50. Organize your walks to get the most out of them, making orderly decisions about pre-walk stretching, diet, shoes (alternate shoes or sneakers for the best foot comfort) and after-walking activities.

Begin by walking for 20 minutes three days a week until your body gets accustomed to it, then build to 30 minutes. Before taking to the streets, limber up the body with stretching exercises for the upper and lower body (see Sports Exercises, page 58, for proper movements), especially if you are just beginning regular walking. Exercises loosen the joints and stretch the muscle fibers to allow them to stretch even further. Without stretching, as you walk your muscles heat up and can tighten, which is counterproductive.

Of course, if you have any foot injury, discontinue walking until it has healed.

Walk at a brisk pace to burn calories. Help this workout by keeping the arms to the side in a natural back-and-forth swing and alternating in direction with the opposite leg. Time your walk or mark the distance, but do the same each time you walk.

talk about
WALKING

- **In the average lifetime, a person travels 70,000 miles on foot.**
- **Your feet are different from each other.**
- **Sometimes just getting rid of a certain pair of shoes can stop the development of a corn or callus.**
- **A blister acts as a natural bandage, protecting an area that has experienced friction.**

Walking shoes or sneakers should be comfortable. You be the judge as to what is comfortable, as long as you consider the proper comfort zones. Ensure sturdy but flexible counters and a flexible sole with soft padding that covers the whole foot. Any heel is not a good idea, because it affects the rhythmic balance of the body's gait.

Consider diet for a walking regimen. You may have seen competition events for which contestants or runners load up on pasta the night before the race. Pasta is a complex carbohydrate (complex of sugar) that breaks down easily in the body, making a quick fuel for endurance. Other good foods are potatoes, rice and beans. Do not use foods like chocolate and candies, because they contain simple sugars, fat and salt that can cause fatigue and swelling.

After a walk, perform additional stretches, similar to pre-walk exercises, but for a shorter time. This helps the joints cool down and relax.

A gentle massage of the feet reduces tightness from a walk. Using circular motions, begin at the toes and work your way up to the heel and ankle, remembering to massage the sole. This loosens the joints and increases circulation to help remove soreness and skin roughness.

For further relief, soak the feet in a solution of Epsom salts either in a pail or a special vibrating foot bath. To treat other parts of the body that cannot be immersed, soak a towel in warm water and wrap it around affected areas; elevate the area using pillows. For the feet, raise them above the heart and rest them on pillows.

Overexertion is bound to happen, and a sure sign is blisters on the feet. The blister--a region of skin that is raised and filled with fluid--is the body's first means of protecting an area that has experienced too much friction. An Epsom salt soak helps blisters too, by drawing out the fluid and even killing some germs. If there is any stinging, soak for a shorter time or dilute the solution.

Do not break or pierce the blister to drain it. A serious local infection may result. If the area is more than a quarter-inch or a half-inch in diameter and is red, open or extremely painful, see a doctor right away.

Index

Decision Tree

for

Sprained Ankle

You have an injury to the ankle:

Can you bear weight?

1. If yes, GO TO PAGE ==> 95

2. If no, GO TO PAGE ==> 96

OR

See Sprained Ankle Flow Chart, page 118

Decision Tree
for
Itchy Feet

You are experiencing itchy feet:

Is there any peeling skin?

(Accompanied or not accompanied by redness)

1. **Yes, there is peeling skin.** **GO TO PAGE ==> 89**

2. **No, there is no peeling skin, but there is redness.** **GO TO PAGE ==> 90**

OR

See Itchy Feet Flow Chart, on page 119

Decision Tree
for
Painful Toenail

You are experiencing a painful toenail:

Is there trauma (injury) to the nail?

1. Yes, there is trauma.

If there is trauma, is it possible to bear weight and move toe?

a. Yes, able to bear weight, and move toe.

GO TO PAGE ==> 101

b. No, not able to bear weight and move toe.

Action: See doctor or professional.

2. No, there is no trauma.

If there is no trauma, is it possible to bear weight and move toe?

a. Yes, able to bear weight, and move toe.

GO TO PAGE ==> 101

b. No, not able to bear weight and move toe.

Action: See doctor or professional.

OR

See Painful Toenail Flow Chart, page 120

Decision Tree
for
Skin Lesions

Is lesion under a bony area, or on top of foot?

1. Yes, under a bony area, or on top of foot. GO TO PAGE ==> 109

2. No, not under a bony area or on top of foot. GO TO PAGE ==> 108

OR

See Skin Lesions Flow Chart, page 121

foot facts Q&A

Is there a root to a corn or a callus that has to be removed for relief?

There is no "root" to the common corn or callus, only a lighter central area where the pain is usually the greatest.

Does a high-calcium diet cause the formation of heel spurs?

No. Calcium formation in a heel spur results from the overuse and constant injury to the heel due to standing and walking.

Can osteoporosis occur in the feet?

Yes. It is common in the elderly to see thinning of the bones—including those of the feet—characteristic of osteoporosis.

How do plantar warts differ from other warts?

"Plantar wart" describes a wart found on the soles of the feet, where the skin is much thicker than elsewhere on the feet, and therefore more resistant to treatment. Plantar warts are usually flat or have indented centers, whereas other warts are elevated from the skin surface. .

When is soaking the feet in hot water advisable?

Never. This would only burn the skin and superficial tendons of the feet.

How do fungal nails form and spread?

Fungi are plantlike organisms that exist mainly in dark, damp, sometimes dirty areas and that can penetrate the nail from the air, water, and on contact with another infected toe or fingernail.

Why may toenails become discolored, hard or ridged?

Nails become brittle with yellow, grainy lines over time due to a condition known as *mycosis,* which is a persistent fungus infection of the nail bed that is difficult to treat.

How can toenails be strengthened so they can grow longer and resist splitting?

If a fungus is causing the weakness or splitting, see a doctor for treatment. But if diet is the culprit, increase your intake of calcium and take a good multiple daily vitamin. Reducing this problem can take between 6 and 12 months.

Are the kinds of corn pads available in stores OK to use?

Only the nonmedicated pads should be used. The caustic ingredient in the other type may cause an infection in corns but can be used on warts if done properly.

Can the toenails be painted with nail polish without fear of infection?

Yes. It is OK to paint the toenails with nail polish, whether they are normal or fungal, irregular or smooth. Using nail polish does not increase the risk of nail disease.

a foot
Glossary

bunion The growth of bone where the big toe meets the forefoot.

bunionette ("tailor's bunion") The growth of bone where the little toe meets the forefoot.

callus A wide expanse of thickened skin, usually on the bottom of the foot.

corn A small area of thickened skin, usually on top of a toe.

forefoot The front part of the foot, including the toes.

gangrene the condition of a part of the body where peripheral vascular disease is so advanced that blood flow has stopped and the flesh is dead or dying.

hammertoe The curling up of a toe other than the big toe.

joint The place at which two bones meet, move and work together.

lesion A generic term for an unusual area of skin.

ligament A soft-tissue structure joining two bones together

muscle A soft-tissue structure joining a bone with the rest of the body to move it in various directions.

neuroma A painful pinched nerve in the forefoot, usually between the third and fourth toes.

onychauxis A greatly thickened nail most often found in older people and caused by a chronic fungus or skin condition.

onycholysis Term describing the separation by trauma of a nail from the nail bed.

onychomycosis A common fungal infection of the nail bed causing the nail to become thick and crusty and fall off in small pieces.

onychomadesis A separating of the nail by trauma in which the nail first separates at the base near the cuticle.

parakeratosis A nonraised skin lesion with the same "footprint" skin lines as the surrounding skin.

pathology The study of diseased parts of the body.

peripheral neuropathy An area of the body where nerves have decreased in their function and as a result experiences numbness and loss of sensitivity.

peripheral vascular disease (PVD) A condition characterized by reduced blood flow to a region, usually as a result of advanced age or diabetes.

pH A measure of the level of acidity or alkalinity. A pH of 7 is neutral, neither acid nor alkaline. A pH less than 7 is acid; a pH greater than 7 is alkaline. The less the pH, the more acidic.

physical therapy The branch of medicine concerned with rehabilitation of the body through deep heat and exercise.

rearfoot The part of the foot from the ankle back to the heel.

reflexology The science of foot massaging of pinpoint areas of the soles thought to help relieve all body pains.

a peek inside the foot-care

Medicine Chest

Here is a suggested first-aid and medicine chest that will let you perform any self-care for foot ailments as outlined in *Foot Facts*.

General Care

Toenail clippers with curved jaw
Straight nail file
Pumice stone for minor calluses and corns
Nonmedicated corn pads for the toes and callus pads for the foot
Utility scissors to cut pads and bandages
Callus-removal tool for minor calluses
Lamb's wool to separate toes in case of friction pain
Toe jackets to cover painful bent toes from top corn pain
Off-the-shelf orthotics for good foot seating in shoes
Vitamin E cream for maintenance of skin health

Emergency Care

Betadine and nonprescription antibiotic cream for minor scrapes
Cold pack for muscle sprains and strains
Elastic ankle brace or Ace bandage for ankle sprains
Tylenol for fever
Motrin for muscle aches and pain
Doughnut pads or heel cups for heel pain
Band Aids, sterile gauze 4 x 4s, adhesive tape, butterfly bandages for closure of deeper wounds
Thermometer (oral, rectal, ear, or forehead strips)
Medicated wart pads to be used as directed
Antifungal cream for minor athlete's foot

Recipes

vinegar (acetic acid): 1-2 oz. per gallon of warm water. Use of white or clear unflavored vinegar.
Clorox (sodium hypochlorite): 1-2 oz. per gallon of warm water.
baking soda (sodium bicarbonate): 1-2 cups per gallon of warm water
Epsom salts (magnesium sulfate): 1-2 cups per gallon of warm water
Betadine (povidone-iodine): 1-2 oz. per gallon of warm water
Tea Bags (tannic acid): 3 bags per gallon of warm water

Dry Recipes for Comfortable Feet

DRYING AGENTS

baking soda

cornstarch

baking powder (a combination of baking soda, cornstarch, calcium phosphate and sodium aluminum sulfate)

talcum powder

baby powder

zinc powder

ANTIFUNGAL AGENTS

undecylenate acid powder (in many products such as Desenex and Caldesene)

Tinactin powder

Lotrimin powder

DRYING AND ANTIFUNGAL

Gold Bond Powder (a commercial formula of menthol, an antifungal, and zinc oxide, a drying agent)

ITCHY FEET, continued:

You have itchy feet, with peeling skin:

Is there any pus or drainage?

1. **Yes, there is pus or draining (and redness).** **GO TO PAGE ==> 93**

2. **No, there is no pus or drainage from skin.** **GO TO PAGE ==> 94**

ITCHY FEET, continued:

You have itchy feet, with some redness, but no peeling skin:

Is there any odor?

1. **Yes, there is odor.** **GO TO NEXT PAGE ==> 91**

2. **No, there is no odor.** **GO TO PAGE ==> 92**

ITCHY FEET, continued:

There is odor.

Possible Mild Athlete's Foot

Action:

1. Use over-the-counter cream, for 2 weeks

2. If no relief, see a doctor or professional.

ITCHY FEET, continued:

There is no odor.

Action: Check shoes for tightness.

See a doctor or professional, as necessary.

ITCHY FEET, continued:

There is pus or drainage (and redness).

Action:

See a doctor or professional.

ITCHY FEET, continued:

There is no pus or drainage from the skin.

Severe Athlete's Foot

Action:

1. **Vinegar pre–soak.**

2. **Over–the–counter cream, for one month.**

3. **If no relief, see a doctor or professional.**

SPRAINED ANKLE, continued:

You have an injured ankle, and can bear weight upon it.

Sprained Ankle

Action: Determine type or level of sprain.

Type I Sprain

Mild or no swelling.

Action: Go to page ==> 97

Type II Sprain

Severe swelling.

Can you move the foot?

1. Yes, can move foot. GO TO PAGE ==> 98
2. No, cannot move foot. GO TO PAGE ==> 99

Type III Sprain

Black & blue; bruised, or open wound; and/or severe swelling or unable to move foot.

Action:

See doctor or professional.

SPRAINED ANKLE, continued:

Ankle injury, and cannot bear weight.

Action: See doctor or professional.

SPRAINED ANKLE, continued:

Type I Ankle Sprain.

Action: for Type I Sprain

1. **Rest:** keep off of foot.
2. **Elevate:** elevate affected limb.
3. **Ice:** ice packs on foot for 20 minutes each hour, off 40 minutes; for 48–72 hours.

Is there improvement, with this management?

1. Yes, there is improvement. GO TO PAGE ==> 100

2. No, there is no improvement.

Action: see doctor or professional.

SPRAINED ANKLE, continued:

Type II Sprain, Able to move foot:

Action: ***Go to Type I Sprain Management, page 97***

SPRAINED ANKLE, continued:

Type II Sprain, Not able to move foot:

Action:

See doctor or professional.

SPRAINED ANKLE, continued:

Type I Sprain, improvement after rest, elevation, ice:

Action:

1. **Epsom salt soaks, for 1 to 2 weeks.**

2. **Exercise limb and muscles.**

PAINFUL TOENAIL, continued:

Pain is present:

Is there nail pain, or only toe pain?

1. There is NAIL pain. GO TO PAGE ==> 103

2. **There is TOE pain, but no nail pain.** **GO TO PAGE ==> 102**

PAINFUL TOENAIL, continued:

TOE pain is present, but NOT nail pain:

Is there pus or drainage present?

1. Yes, there is pus or drainage

   Action: See Doctor or Professional

1. No, there is no pus or drainage

   Action: GO TO PAGE ==> 105

PAINFUL TOENAIL, continued:

NAIL pain is present:

Is there pus?

1. Yes, there is pus. GO TO PAGE ==> 104

2. No, there is no pus. GO TO PAGE ==> 105

PAINFUL TOENAIL, continued:
NAIL pain is present, there is PUS present:

Action:

1. Vinegar soaks.

2. Massage toenail borders.

GO TO PAGE ==> 106

PAINFUL TOENAIL, continued:

NAIL pain, but no pus:

Action:

1. Epsom salt soaks.

2. Massage toe borders.

GO TO PAGE ==> 107

PAINFUL TOENAIL, continued:

Is there improvement in 2 days?

If no improvement in 2 days,

See doctor or professional.

PAINFUL TOENAIL, continued:

Is there improvement in 7 days?

If no improvement in 7 days,

See doctor or professional.

SKIN LESIONS, continued

Skin lesion under a bony area:

Lesion is painful on lateral pressure,

but

Does toenail show pinpoint bleed on trimming?

1. Yes, pinpoint bleeding on trimming. GO TO PAGE ==> 111

2. No, no pinpoint bleeding on trimming. GO TO PAGE ==> 110

SKIN LESIONS, continued

Skin lesion, not directly under bony area or on top of foot:

Is the lesion painful to pressure?

1, Yes, lesion is painful to direct pressure. GO TO PAGE ==> 113

2. No, lesion is not painful on any pressure. GO TO PAGE==> 114

SKIN LESIONS, continued
No pinpoint bleeding when trimmed:

Parakeratosis

Action

See doctor or professional.

SKIN LESIONS, continued

Pinpoint bleeding when trimmed:

Is the lesion larger than a pencil eraser?

1. Yes, larger than a pencil eraser.

Action:

See doctor or professional.

2. No, not larger than a pencil eraser. GO TO PAGE ==> 112

SKIN LESIONS, continued

No, lesion not larger than pencil eraser:

WART

Action:

1. Acid patches.
2. If no improvement in 14 days, see doctor or professional.

SKIN LESIONS, continued

Skin lesion painful to direct pressure:

Is lesion on toe, or on foot?

1. **TOE:**

   Diagnosis: Corn

   Action: 1. Trim at home.

   2. If no relief, see doctor or professional.

2. **FOOT:**

   Diagnosis: Callus

   Action: 1. Trim at home.

   2. If no relief, see doctor or professional.

SKIN LESIONS, continued

Skin lesion, not painful on any pressure:

Is there any itching?

1. Yes, itching is present. GO TO PAGE ==> 115

2. No, there is no itching. GO TO PAGE ==> 116

SKIN LESIONS, continued

Skin lesion, with itching:

Action: Distinguish kind of itching skin lesion.

1. Silvery borders.

   Diagnosis: Psoriasis

   Action: Hydrocortisone cream

   If no relief in 7 days, see doctor or professional.

2. Outlined shape.

   Diagnosis: Allergic dermatitis

   Action: Hydrocortisone cream

   If no relief in 7 days, see doctor or professional.

3. Blotchy patches.

   Diagnosis: Poison ivy / Poison oak

   Action: Hydrocortisone cream

   If no relief in 7 days, see doctor or professional.

SKIN LESIONS, continued

Skin lesion, without itching:

ATOPIC DERMATITIS

Action:

1. Hydrocortisone cream
2. If no relief in 7 days, see doctor or professional.

APPENDIX

Flow Charts

Sprained Ankle Flow Chart

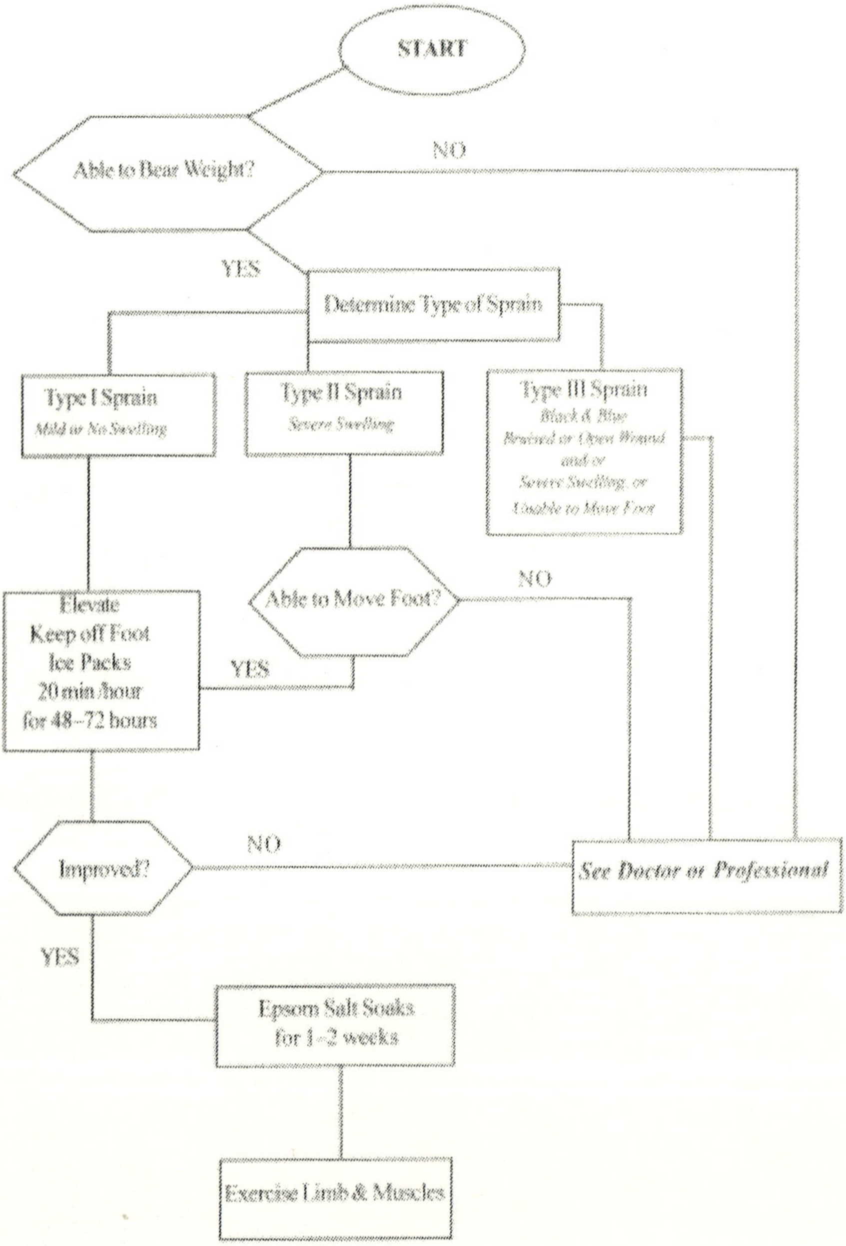

Itchy Feet Flow Chart

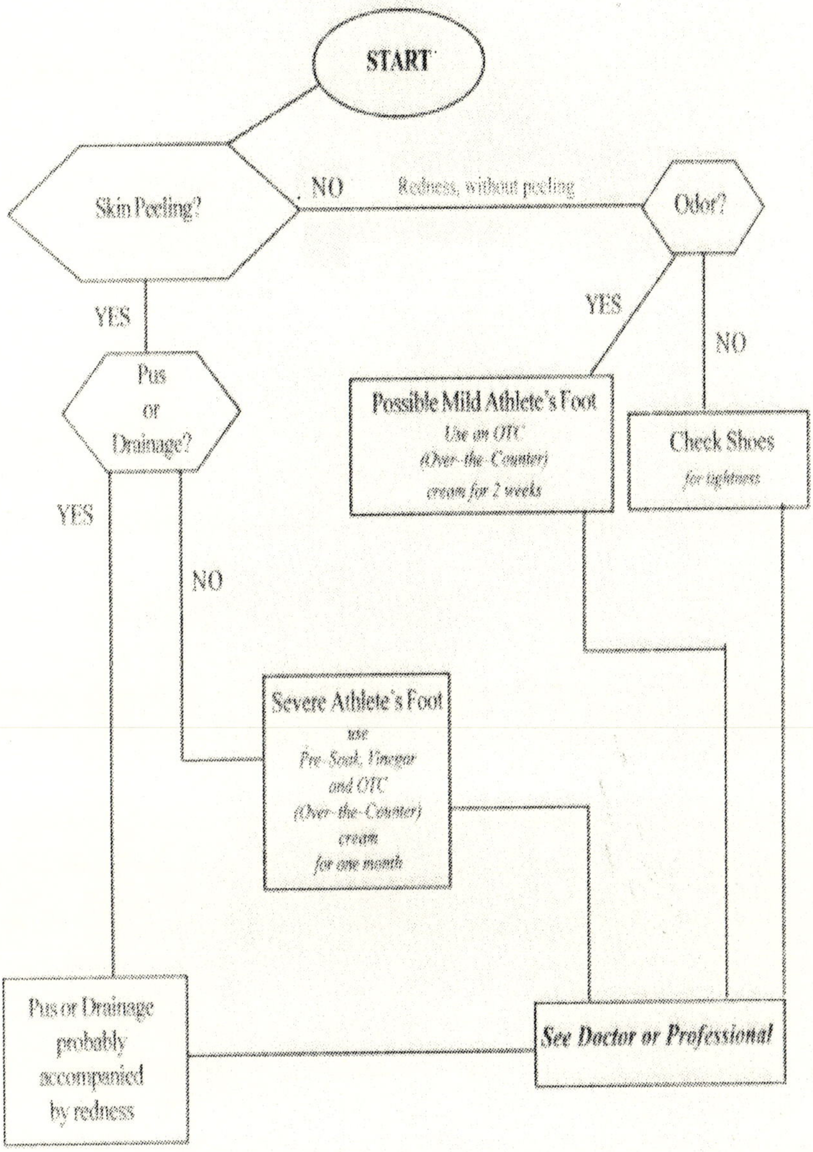

Painful Toenail Flow Chart

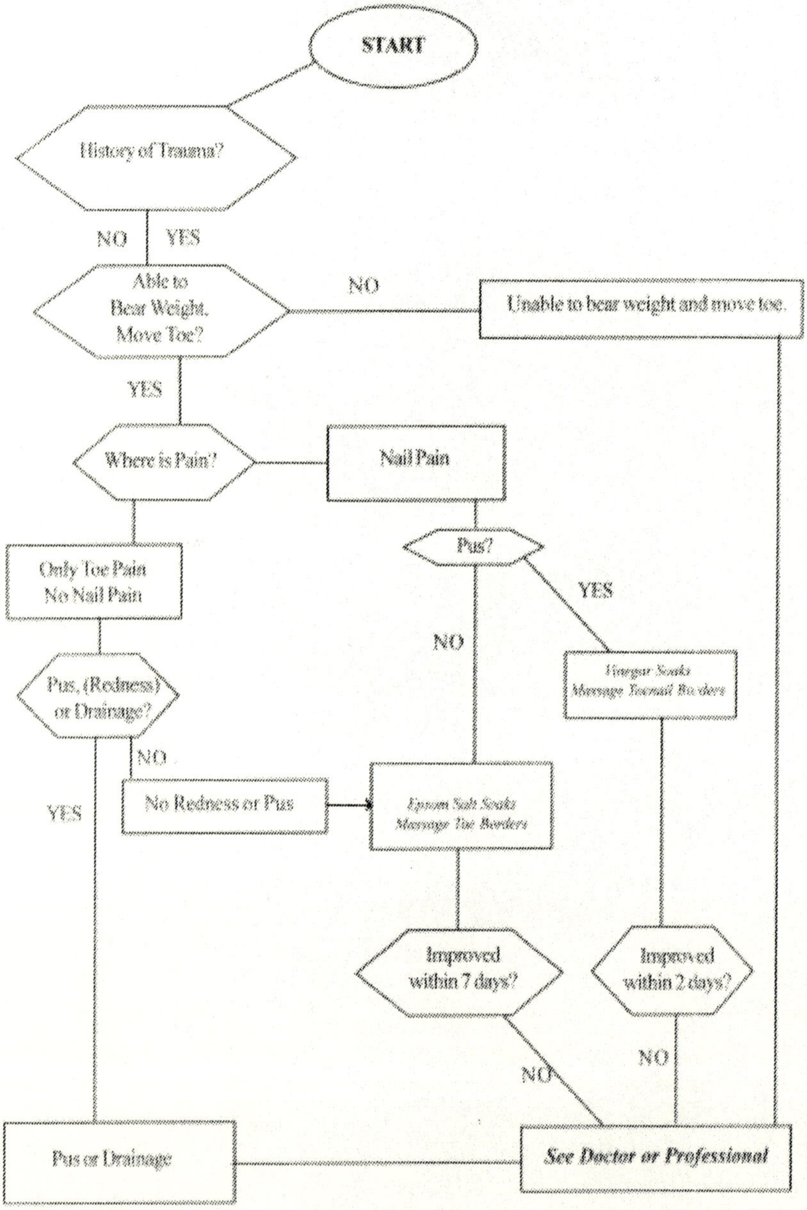

60

Skin Lesions Flow Chart

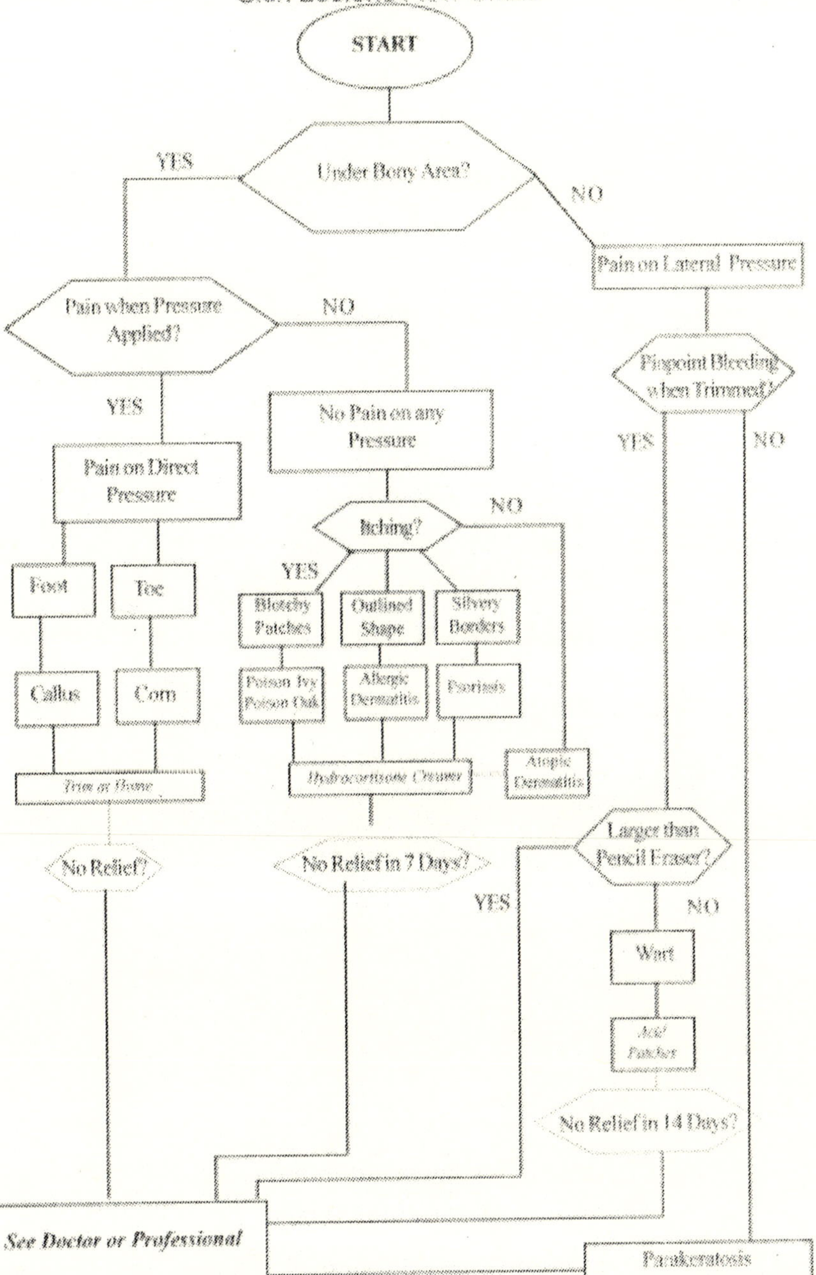

Printed in the United States
880100002BB

9 781883 938963